STUDY ADVICE FOR GEOGRAPHY A-LEVEL

Edited by
Norman Law
With Michael Witherick

Contributors: David Elcome
Garrett Nagle
Murray Thomas
Sue Warn
Michael Witherick

Series Editor:
Michael Witherick

Stanley Thornes (Publishers) Ltd

First published in 1998 by:
Stanley Thornes (Publishers) Ltd
Ellenborough House
Wellington Street
CHELTENHAM GL50 1YW
England

98 99 00 01 02 / 10 9 8 7 6 5 4 3 2 1

A catalogue record for this book is available from the British Library.

ISBN 0-7487-3184-9

Designed by Giles Davies
Page layout and illustration by Hardlines, Charlbury, Oxford
Cover design by Sterling Associates
Cover photograph: Courtesy IBM

Printed and bound in Great Britain by Martins The Printers Ltd, Berwick upon Tweed

Contents

Introduction

SECTION A

The idea behind this book

The preparation of this book has been based on four key principles:

- the book should incorporate advice given by people with considerable experience as A-level examiners or sixth-form teachers
- there should be a major input from students currently studying A-level Geography and from those who have recently passed the examination
- it should include topics that A-level Geography students have indicated they want covered
- it should be organised and written in a style that students find easy to use.

In order to satisfy the second and third principles, the preparation of this book has involved considerable research and consultation with both present A-level students and students who have recently completed their courses. In other words, it has tried hard to identify:

- those aspects of A-level Geography with which students feel they most need help
- the best ideas from recent A-level Geography students, in particular those things that helped them most
- the ways in which this help can best be delivered.

We have already illustrated, in fact, one of the students' main demands. They wanted easy checklists and bullet-point summaries wherever possible. They also asked for the book to be easy to read, to cut the jargon and not to be patronising. To ensure that this last requirement was met, we recruited a team of student advisors and asked them to make suggestions and edit the text so that we were sure it met with their approval. The names of these advisors are listed in the Acknowledgements (page 111), and we are very grateful to them for their valuable input.

There is rarely only one 'right' way of doing things, and that includes how to study Geography at A-level. In fact, students should be encouraged to find their own best way of working; shall we call it your **optimum way of learning (OWL)**. However, pooling and analysing many years of experience have ensured that this book provides a framework around which an individual can create an effective learning and revision programme. Such a programme may be expected to have three key outcomes:

- enjoyment of the subject
- confidence in personal abilities
- examination success.

SECTION B

How to use this book

One of the most important messages of the book is the one just outlined. You should lose no time in discovering what is your own **OWL. Chapter 2** suggests various possibilities. We know that everyone's circumstances are different. Some of you will be working in a room full of other people, perhaps listening to music or with one eye on the television. Some others will be working quietly in a study, library, bedroom or a corner of the living-room. Those circumstances are often difficult to change. So we need to ensure that you make the best of them that you can. The techniques outlined in this book will help you to do just this.

The chapters that follow the search for your OWL are specifically designed to help you write better essays and short answers, to take better notes, to draw better diagrams, to learn more effectively and to cope better with many other important aspects of your A-level work. Each of these chapters can be taken separately. You do not need to work your way through the book from beginning to end. The book is your companion to be used as best suits you.

SECTION C

Anxious about the new course?

Many of our student advisors told us that one of the most difficult things they had to cope with was the transfer from GCSE to A-level. Some found it very easy and you may be one of these happy people. However, the transfer certainly involves changing up a gear. You will be working at a higher intellectual level; you will be expected to show more knowledge and understanding. It may also require a change in the way you study. For sure, the start of the new course can be a worrying and stressful time. It is very natural to question whether geography was after all the right subject for you and to doubt whether you can cope with the demands of the course. The best way we can help here is to list some strategies that have been used successfully by past A-level students to overcome this tricky transition.

- Don't worry, as nearly everyone goes through such a phase. By the end of the first half-term break, most of you will be wondering what you were worried about. Talk to some students who have been on the course for some time. Find out how they coped.
- Ask the teacher for guidance on how you can best get into the course. We know that students don't like to admit they are finding things difficult as they think it might count against them. So put your request positively, for example: 'What might I do to improve the way I am working?' It may well be that by asking in this way you will be able to prioritise what you should be doing.
- As early as you can, get hold of a summary of the examination syllabus and, if you have the nerve, perhaps look at some previous examination papers. You will then have a clearer idea of where you are heading.
- Take action to improve some simple learning and study techniques. Many are suggested in this book.

If you did but know it, virtually everyone on your course is feeling anxious about the transfer. Some will not worry too much. Others (probably most) will worry quite a lot but not let on. We hope you will find some reassurance here and be encouraged to approach your work in a more confident and positive frame of mind. It is vital that you take action to help yourself. Using this book is one such way. It has a number of benefits to offer.

- It is full of tried and tested tips – they actually work.
- Our student advisors have told us that it is easy to read.
- It urges you to find your own 'best way' of working before you do anything else.
- It will help you with most of the basic activities involved in the A-level course, from note-taking to improving examination technique, from essay writing to planning a personal enquiry. There is no need to read the book from cover to cover in one go. Use it on an 'as and when' basis.
- Use of the techniques and tips will increase your confidence. A confident student is a happy one. A happy student usually has a positive outlook. Such a sequence may be expected to lead to examination success.

CHAPTER

2 Learning to learn

SECTION A

Discover your OWL

Library shelves are full of books telling you things like work in a quiet room, spend at least one hour on a subject each day, write notes in a particular way, etc. Whilst this may be well intended and in some cases helpful advice, such generalisations will not suit everyone. Each student is an individual and therefore in a sense different. For example, various aspects of family life and the home environment can be powerfully influential when it comes to studying. Not everyone has the benefit of adults in the house who can help with their work, quiet space in the home for study or access to a word processor. Students also differ in terms of significant personal qualities such as concentration span, learning capacity, motivation, personality and temperament. In short, there are a thousand and one different things that have a bearing on what constitutes a student's **optimum way of learning (OWL)** – the acronym is appropriate given the legendary wisdom of this bird!

Discovering your OWL basically involves finding sound answers to three questions.

- **When** – at what times of the day and on what days do you feel that you work best?
- **Where** – in which locations at school, at home and elsewhere do you find it easiest to study?
- **How** – what methods of learning suit you best and how do you make your mind most receptive to new knowledge and understanding?

In the vast majority of cases, it is you the student who is best qualified to answer these questions and to arrive at a way of studying that suits you well and that is most likely to produce the best results. It is preferable for you to discover and define your own OWL rather than be forced to follow a model of 'perfect' or 'universal' practice. The latter could be wholly unsuited to your particular circumstances, personality and character. The sooner you discover your OWL the better – at the beginning of your course rather than well into it. Once you have found it, stick with it, but do not be frightened to review it occasionally and perhaps refine it.

Perhaps you should be left on your own to find the answers to the first two OWL questions of 'when' and 'where'. You might welcome some help with the third question of 'how', however. Here are some pieces of basic advice.

SECTION B

Think positively

From the outset, it is vitally important in any learning situation that you put yourself in the right frame of mind. It is all too easy to start thinking negatively. This is the most important thing to recognise and deal with early on in the course. You have been accepted on an A-level Geography course. You are already, therefore, in the top 10 per cent of the UK population so far as the subject is concerned. Your work has been judged to be of a high quality by an external examiner. You are a success. Okay, you might find the change from GCSE to A-level a difficult one; you would be a very unusual case if you did not. You might also get lower marks than you hoped for in some of the essays you write during the A-level course.

The trick is to remain focused on success rather than uncertainty. You are, after all, on the course to learn. If you were not to make any mistakes at all along the way, there would be no need to be on the course in any case. As Kipling said, success and failure are the two certain components of anyone's existence. You just have to learn to deal with the 'two imposters' in the same manner so that, in the end, your ability and hard work shine through. Let's have a look at a few ways in which we can help in this respect.

First, complete the following self-appraisal.

Review

1 Make a list of your strong points – we do not want to know about your weaknesses. Focus on your strengths. The list might run something like this:

- I am easy to talk to.
- I make friends easily.
- I am good at tennis and intend to improve my game.
- I like helping other people.
- I want to be a success.

There's nothing here about academic work! But anyone could be proud of such a list. Compiling the list has encouraged you to focus on positive aspects of your character. It sets the scene for you to do well. There is no need to share your list with anyone else. Hide it away if you want to, but take a pride in it (that is, assuming that it is truthful and accurate).

This list also shows that such a person is able to share ideas with others, has ambition, is able to focus on a specific area (tennis in this case) and relates well to other people. In short, what is revealed here is a good foundation of personal qualities on which to base academic success.

Once you have identified your strong points, gradually try to exploit them in your A-level work. For example, you may have said that you are easy to talk to and make friends easily. So why not take advantage of this and open up a co-operative dialogue with others in your class. For example, you might exchange thoughts about the next essay – points to be made, where to find suitable case-study material, useful references and so on.

SECTION C

Set goals and rewards

A good way to reinforce a positive approach to your studies is to think about what you are trying to do in the subject. This can be achieved by checking your **goals** every so often.

Goals are targets; things to be aimed at. In this case, they should be achievable and measurable. In other words, don't ask too much of yourself, but be able to know when you have achieved them. The table **2.1** shows how you might set them out at the start of your A-level course.

Figure 2.1 My goals (written on 1 September)

In the ...	Goal	Target date
SHORT TERM, I will...	List my positive points	by the end of the first week.
	Draw up a study timetable showing how I intend to allocate my 'free' time both at school and at home to each of my subjects	by the end of the second week.
MEDIUM TERM, I will...	Find out what is required of me when I write my first A-level essay	by the end of the third week.
	Buy a recommended course textbook	by the end of the fourth week.
	Define my OWL	by half-term.
LONG TERM, I will...	Prove to myself that I have made the right choice of subject	by the end of the Christmas term.
	Be up to date with my class notes and reading	by the end of the Christmas holiday.

Review

2 Compile a list of achievable short-, medium- and long-term goals in your study of Geography. If you have any problem in identifying goals at these different time-scales, have a chat to a few friends about it, or even talk to your teacher. By the way, it is a good way of signalling your intentions to your teacher. It is remarkable how the image created by such a positive act feeds back into the way you are regarded by teachers. Try it!

Goals such as those shown in **2.1** do not ask too much of the student. There are not too many of them and they are achievable. There are clear dates by which the student can see whether they have been addressed or not. They can be continuously updated.

- If you work towards an achievable goal, you can build up your own self-esteem and satisfaction. You will have no need of anyone else to tell you how you are doing.
- You will also help to bolster your own self-confidence, which is fundamental to doing well on your course.

In business, if you set goals and they are achieved, you often get rewards. Why not borrow this idea? We all know some lucky devils who get a mountain bike for passing exams. We're not talking about that. We are talking about personal rewards to reinforce good work as you progress through the course.

If you are trying to learn a case study, for example, test yourself until you are sure you have learned it (we'll give you some more help on this later in the book) and then give yourself a reward. This could be a break to listen to a few tracks from a CD, a trip to the kitchen to get a snack, a phone call to a friend – the list is endless. The reward does not have to be huge, but it allows you to focus on the task at hand and ensures that you have achieved it. Make sure, however, that the reward does not get in the way. If you find that you are not concentrating on your work, try another technique.

Review

Give yourself rewards.

3 When you complete a task in a given time, achieve a good grade, improve your understanding of a difficult topic or complete a tidying session with your notes, give yourself some sort of small treat. This will reinforce your good habits and build up a positive image of yourself. Don't under-estimate the power of this little trick – but don't be too easy with your rewards or you will devalue them.

SECTION D

Get out of your own way

In a delightful little book by J. J. Gibbs, *Dancing with Your Books – the Zen Way of Studying* (Plume/Penguin Group, 1990), the author argues that it is not what you are learning or even the tricks you use to learn more effectively that are most important. It is the way that you approach the whole business of learning. He tells his students to 'get out of your own way'. He goes on to say:

> *... learning does not have to be a chore. Much of the pain, anguish and discomfort associated with schoolwork is unnecessary and avoidable ... The process of learning not only can be just as enjoyable as the results, but also it makes good sense to focus more on the process than results.*

Just think about it for a minute. For instance, how often has your mind wandered whilst doing your homework? Perhaps you have felt that you were not getting on very well with it. Perhaps you were wishing that you were doing something else. Perhaps you felt that the homework was pointless and that the examination would allow you to prove that you knew it all anyway. But why are you having thoughts such as these? One explanation suggested by Gibbs is that you have not understood the process of learning. A vital part of that process is knowing how to focus on the work in front of us. Gibbs claims:

> *Although it sounds bizarre, I think the biggest problem most students face is getting out of their own way so their natural intelligence can do the work it is supposed to do unencumbered.*

In other words, don't let negative and random thoughts distract you from realising your potential. The best way to rid yourself of this handicap is to approach your learning in a positive way, rather than as a slave having to complete a task in a given time. Gibbs' recommendation, which may well appeal to many students, is to apply the principles of Zen. Zen teaches that people should live fully in the present, letting each new experience enrich them. It also teaches how to recognise and discard the awkward, negative baggage that we often carry with us. Once this is done, then people are able to get the most out of what they are doing at any one time.

Whilst we offer this as one way in which students could find their OWL, we understand that not all are going to relate to the Zen way of doing things. It does, however, teach us some very important lessons.

- Recognise how you learn most effectively.
- Be single-minded in giving yourself the conditions under which you learn best.
- The most important of all of these is to believe in your own ability.
- Focus on the present – the past has gone, the future is unknown. Make sure that you use the present to its full potential.

Let us now concentrate on the last of these four lessons. How do we get out of our own way and concentrate better on what we are doing? There are several techniques (apart from Zen) which have been used successfully by a variety of people to achieve this.

All of us are very busy. We have things we like doing, which we would like to do more. Equally we have things we dislike, which we would like to avoid. A-level study, essay writing and note-making may well fit into the second category for a lot of people. A conscious effort must be made to put your A-level work into the former category by zooming in on those aspects of your course that appeal most.

It may be that we feel we 'haven't got time' to do something. If this is the case then we may well panic and probably do a rushed or incomplete job, blaming our 'lack of time' for the inevitable result. But surely if we have made the decision to study for A-levels (probably with the justification of improving job chances, going to university or giving ourselves more time to make the decision about what to do next), we owe it to ourselves to find the time to do the job properly.

SECTION E

Manage your time

There is an old saying that 'if a job is worth doing, it's worth doing well'. The key here is **time management**. Amongst all the other things you are doing, you must decide positively and for yourself that you will use certain blocks of time for your subject.

It is a mistake to think that you must only do what your teacher asks you to do in the subject. **You** know best whether or not you have enough knowledge and understanding. If you have identified areas of weakness in either of these, you need to devote some extra time to improve them (we suggest how you might do this later in the book). So you need to free up blocks of time for each of your subjects, including Geography. This time should have the following characteristics.

- It should enable you to concentrate on the job at hand, without interference from other demands.
- It should be long enough to enable you to complete the task, or part of it, to a high standard.
- It should not be so long in one go that you begin to work inefficiently, start thinking about other things or get bored.

Review

4 What are you going to do over the next week in Geography? When are you going to do it? Write it down and, having worked through it, review the way you did it. After a while, you will have an efficient means of planning your time and checking on your progress.

We are not going to suggest how long these sessions should be. You are sensible enough to find your own answer. The one thing you must do, however, is to make a promise to yourself to stick with your plan. You may use the time in different ways later on, but make the time available in the first place.

Some people work by writing out a time-planner in a diary, perhaps one week in advance. Others work on a daily basis, ensuring that the various subjects get a fair share of time. Whichever way they do it, consistency is the thing. We hear about good habits – these are what give people their character. Good habits make good character and this is one of the things on which you will be selected for college entrance, training or a job. Habits are simply strategies adopted by an individual and repeated again and again. One of the smartest is the good use of time. Make it one of your priorities to use your time effectively. If you plan your time wisely, you will develop useful aspects of your character and set yourself up for life.

Here are some other ways of planning the use of your time.

Avoid promising too much

If you make a list of how much time in every 24 hours you spend on sleeping, eating, travelling, watching TV, resting, taking part in sports or hobbies etc. you will soon get an idea of what is available to you for your own work. This will give you an idea of what is a realistic amount you can give over to studying. You might be surprised how little time there is and how well you must therefore use it.

Don't waste time

You may have been tempted to put some unusual things on your list that really have a much lower priority than some of the others. At any time in the course you may decide that you have not got the right information to do the job properly, that you can't concentrate or that you can do it tomorrow. Recognise that all of these are excuses – easy ways out of doing what you should be doing. Deal with them firmly and tell yourself that you have set the time aside for Geography, so even if you really cannot do what you had intended to do, you want to do something else to help your development in the subject. This might include watching a TV documentary, reading the

Review

Have you got any other smart ideas about time management?

5 The ones covered here have been mentioned by our student advisors, but they are not the only ones. Talk to your friends about ways they have found to organise their time well. Incorporate the ideas you like best into your own strategy.

newspaper or thinking about a particular topic. Stay focused on success in the subject by identifying and throwing out the excuses.

Work to deadlines

You may have been given a date for handing in an essay. Many students will be writing it the day before it is due in. Don't be one of them. Plan in enough time after 'finishing' the essay to check it through or to sort out any problems that you might have encountered. Set yourself deadlines for your own personal note-making sessions (and don't forget to reward yourself for meeting them).

Use 'dead' time

Everyone has time when they are waiting for a bus or train or actually travelling, which could be used rather than wasted. Then there is that unexpected 'free' time – perhaps the teacher is away or you are snowed in. Be prepared to use this time constructively to improve your knowledge or understanding. No time should be 'dead'. If you must, decide to use it for relaxation, but stay positive. If you start to feel that you are wasting time then you will start to get negative thoughts which will not help at all.

SECTION F

Listening

During your course, you will be expected to listen to a wide variety of inputs. These will include lectures from your teachers, class discussions and TV or radio presentations. They will all demand that you listen carefully in order to receive and understand the information.

Before we come on to note-making, which is capturing the essential details from these (and written) sources, we must focus on **how** to listen. This skill is very simple, but often overlooked. Really it boils down to conscious concentration on the task at hand. Try to forget thoughts such as 'this is too complicated' or the even more destructive 'this is boring'. Think instead that 'somewhere in this, there is probably an idea that will gain me an extra mark or two in my exams'. That way, your expectations are not too high but you are searching for the golden nugget. Here are a few more suggestions for better listening.

- **Clear your mind** of other thoughts and concentrate on the medium you are listening to. Approach the task positively.
- **Be active** (not passive) in your listening. Listen **for** something rather than **at** something. Ask questions in your mind as you listen. Don't just let the information wash over you.
- **Create a framework** within which to listen.
  – What is the main idea contained in the information?
  – What evidence is quoted to support that idea?

- What links does it have with your existing knowledge?
- Listen for stresses. This helps you to prioritise the importance of points made.

- **Summarise** the information you have gathered in your notes.

Effective listening may be seen therefore as involving four basic steps (**TLQR**).

- **Tune in** – take a conscious decision to rid your mind of other thoughts and concentrate on the task at hand.
- **Listen** – this requires that you hear what is being said at its face value and that you do not make any sort of subjective or emotional judgement (that comes later).
- **Question** – while you are listening, constantly ask yourself what points are being made.
- **Review** – this is the note-making, revision and evaluative process after the listening session.

By appreciating these simple guidelines and by applying them as suits you best, you can radically improve your listening ability. Since listening well is fundamental to your success at this level, it is worth making a conscious effort to improve your listening skills.

SECTION G

Reading

This is perhaps the main source of your information on an advanced course, but it is another of those skills that is often taken for granted and not reviewed. A small amount of time taken to concentrate on improving your reading skills pays handsome dividends.

A text is always read in a context. If you get this context under control, you can learn a lot more from what you read. The following may well limit the rate at which you read.

- The material itself (size of print, presence or absence of illustrations, clarity of style, relevance of topic, etc.).
- Your perception of its importance. Do you say 'I've got to read this' or do you say 'This might just contain the information I'm looking for'?
- Your existing knowledge. Is the topic new to you or do you have some background information to help you to understand it?
- The circumstances. What are your surroundings like? Are you rushing to get on to something else? What is the lighting like?

Ensure, first of all, that you address each of these points and approach the new text in a positive frame of mind. Now, how can you read it more quickly and, at the same time, more efficiently?

Just as in listening, the first thing you ought to do is to set a goal. For a reading session, it might be (short-term) to gather some relevant information for an essay. The long-term goal might be to develop a detailed case study for potential use in an examination. Once that is clear, which of the following 'bad' reading habits would you admit to?

- Pronouncing words to yourself as you read.
- Going back to re-read a passage already covered.
- Stopping to stare at a particular word.
- Losing your place or wandering between lines.

All of these are signs of undisciplined reading. You may have noticed how towards the end of a novel, when your interest is at its greatest, you seldom, if ever, have any of these faults. Here is a routine that can help you to 'speed read' and improve your understanding at the same time. It is not a magic formula, however, and it needs a lot of practice to get it right. You should set out to understand what you read, not to memorise it.

Review

How to 'speed read'

6
- Turn the pages with your left hand. Run the relaxed fingers of your right hand down the edge of the page you are reading, pulling your eyes down the page with them. Take about three seconds to scan one page.
- Focus on a wide band down the centre of the page. Do not try to read every word. Instead, try to get the sense of what is being said. Concentrate on as many words as possible, but do not read individual words.
- Tell yourself what you have read on the page.
- Now try it on several pages consecutively, taking about three seconds per page.

Don't forget that reading is a vital skill. If you take a few minutes each day to practise this, you will have a valuable skill not only for your examination course, but for life. There are many specialised books available on speed reading if you want to know more. There is a very useful section, for example, in *Student Success Secrets* by Eric Jensen, published by Barrons in 1996.

SECTION H

Making notes

There are lots of techniques mentioned in this book to help with your note-making. They include concept mapping, mind mapping, various forms of diagram and sketch map, and revision cards. Your notebooks should be well organised so that you can easily find material relating to particular topics. Every time you write notes, remind yourself that you are doing it for a purpose. This will enable you to revise efficiently and consequently do well in the examinations.

You have probably heard the saying 'variety is the spice of life'. Variety helps to spice up your notes as well and make them more memorable. Here are a few techniques you can use to ensure that your notes are stimulating and easy to use.

- Try to summarise, where possible, with sketches, diagrams or other illustrations. Don't simply repeat what you are told. Put it in your own words.
- Make notes as relevant to you as possible. Add the occasional personal comment if you like. Develop your own style.
- Use different colours for the main headings, side headings and key terms. This makes them more visually appealing.
- Try different styles of note-making. Some notes you might summarise in bullet-point form. Others you might write in more detail. Which works better for you?
- Design your notes to draw in all your emotions. Use coloured margins, thought bubbles, comments from newspapers, sketches, etc. Be inventive.
- File them well, perhaps under section headings such as physical geography, urban geography, etc.

Once you have experimented and found a style of note-making that suits you, stay with it. Some people find this the single most difficult part of transferring to A-level. There is a great temptation to write down everything, but this should be resisted at all costs. In fact, you might try spending most of your time listening rather than writing. As you read (or listen) just note down any key terms (with their definitions) and main ideas. Obviously, you should copy any sketches or diagrams used if they sum up key points. Copy up your notes afterwards, fleshing them out from your understanding rather than your memory. Once again, aim to develop your own style and then stick to it.

SECTION I

A learning model

Learning does not just happen. In any well-structured lesson there are a number of stages through which learning comes about. In other words, there is a strategy behind the process of learning. Very often the process involves the following steps or stages.

1 What is already known?

The teacher will talk briefly about the subject, perhaps asking questions about it to establish a mental picture and to know where to begin. For example, the lesson might be about volcanoes. 'Has anyone ever visited a place where there are volcanoes?' might be the opening question. If there was a positive answer, the next one might be: 'Could you describe it for me?' The student replying might be asked to draw a sketch of the volcano and the rest of the group might then be asked about the names given to various parts of it.

After a short series of questions such as this, the teacher will know where to start from before going into more detail about volcanoes. It may be that the pupils already know about the distribution of volcanoes around the globe.

Review

Following the five-stage sequence.

7 When you come to a new topic, be clear in your own mind:

- what you already know about the topic
- what the objectives are in the study of that topic
- what information to record, and how
- how best to check your grasp of the topic
- how the topic links with other parts of the subject.

2 What is the learning objective?

From this point, the teacher will have a clear idea of what the class understanding is now and what it should be by the end of the lesson. The objective in this instance might be to understand and explain the distribution they already know about.

3 What information is to be recorded and how?

You will need to make notes, of course, but in a form that will enable you to revise easily. Are there any other materials that could be used to ensure that a full understanding is achieved – an annotated diagram of constructive and destructive plate margins, for example?

4 Has the topic been properly understood?

This may be checked out in a number of different ways – by a session of short oral questions and answers, a class discussion or an essay-type question. For the student, self-assessment is best achieved by going through notes and carefully checking that everything is understood.

5 How does what you have learned relate to other parts of the subject?

Learning works on the instalment plan. New pieces of knowledge are added, but unless you are very careful you could end up with just a bagful of bits. There is a need to understand that subjects have cohesion and that each small topic has a context. Furthermore, it is often the case that the same broad principles emerge in the study of different topics.

Let's now look at an example to illustrate this sequence. This example reviews the formation of a sea stack following the process outlined above.

Step 1 What do you know about coastal erosion? Where have you visited that has some good examples of eroding cliffs? Or can you name some examples from books you have read or programmes/films you have seen? Can you name an example of a sea stack? (You might look at *Environment and People* page 55 to help you.)

Step 2 The objective is to understand how the sea stack has been formed within the context of coastal development.

Step 3 The notes should convey the following sequence of development; a diagram would also help (**2.2**).

A cave is formed at high water mark where a line of weakness in the cliff meets incoming waves. The line of weakness could be a joint, a fault or a different rock type, for example. The waves hitting this point may

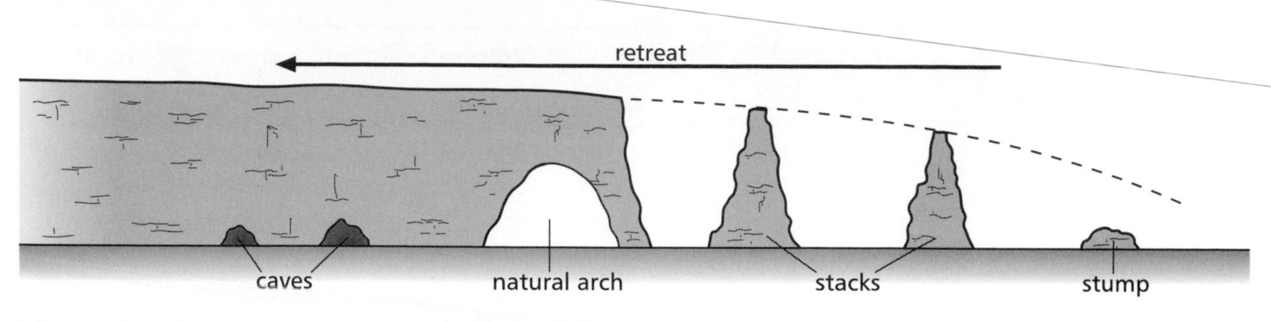

Figure 2.2 The retreat of a headland

compress the air trapped in the joint. When this air is released as the wave recedes, the pressure difference may be very sudden. After thousands of repetitions of this cycle, the rock may crumble. The process described is known as hydraulic action and it is a common process of marine erosion.

The wave may also pick up pebbles and throw them at the cliff, having most effect where the rock is weakest. This is known as abrasion. In addition, the corrosive action of the sea water may have most effect along the line of weakness where the water can be in touch with a larger surface area.

*By all of these means, the rock can be eroded and a cave formed. In a headland, this may take place from either side , leading to the formation of a cave which is drilled right through, resulting in a feature known as an arch (**2.2**). Finally, the arch roof may collapse, leaving a sea stack separated from the main headland.*

To this explanatory account, you might include in your notes a few examples of coastlines being eroded in this way, as well as the names of some caves, arches and stacks.

Step 4 Checking that you have understood the formation of sea stacks might be done in a number of different way. For example, you might draw **2.2** from memory and write on it numbered annotations to explain the development sequence. Equally, you could take the role of teacher and explain the sequence to a friend.

Step 5 Diagram **2.2** serves to underline the important point that whilst the sea stack is a unique feature, all sea stacks are formed in the same general way. Figure **2.3** on page 20 broadens the view by suggesting that the formation of other geomorphological features is influenced by many of the same factors and often by the same process. Furthermore, recognition that the sea stack is simply one component of a much larger system (the coast) also helps bind this particular topic to the body of physical geography. All this constitutes what is known as **context**, which is vitally important.

Figure 2.3 How landforms are created

Factors ⇨ (influence) ⇨	**Process** ⇨ (which gives) ⇨	**Form**
rock type altitude climate soil vegetation animals people	coastal erosion	sea stack

Review

8 Compile a detailed list of the factors influencing the formation of a desert sand dune. What main process is involved in this case?

9 Look at any other landform described in *Environment and People* (e.g. the arête, page 78) and explain how it is formed.

10 What common elements do you find in these two enquiries and the formation of a sea stack?

Hopefully, you can now see how understanding the process of learning helps greatly in your ability to learn and understand the facts. **Chapter 3** takes us through some individual study and learning techniques that build on the ground just covered.

SECTION J

Summing up

Effective learning involves laying a firm foundation of good practice.

- Organise your time well from early in the course. Set targets and, if you achieve them, reward yourself.
- Practise the key skills of listening, reading and note-making. Do not take them for granted. They are initially much more important than any geographical content.
- Subject each new exercise or topic to a sequence of questions:
  - What do you already know on this topic?
  - What precisely do you hope to add to that knowledge?
  - What information do you need to collect?
  - How are you going to ensure that you have actually learned it?
- Don't learn anything in a vacuum. Try to see how it is related to other parts of the subject.
- Allow enough time to be able to learn the subject thoroughly.
- Pick out the best approach for you and stick with it.

All this advice should be incorporated as a basic part of your OWL.

CHAPTER

3

Techniques for better learning and revision

The aim of this chapter is to suggest some ways in which you might improve your learning. If they suit you, then they should become part of your **OWL**. The same techniques should also prove useful in the context of revising for the exams that lie at the end of your module or course.

SECTION A

Mind mapping

You will find that the mind-mapping technique is extremely useful in many situations, but especially when you are trying to learn new information. Diagram **3.1** is a simple mind map showing how a party might be organised. The person who drew it up decided on all the most important aspects (food, music, parking, invitations, drink, clearing up) and then wrote points linked to each of them so that, hopefully, everything was thought of. How might we apply this to Geography?

Figure 3.1 A mind map for organising a party

An example

Let us say that you are trying to learn the key points about the uses and problems of the motor car. In order to provide a coherent starting point, carry out a personal 'brainstorm', jotting down your ideas as they occur on a large piece of paper, perhaps A3 size. On it you are going to make a mind map showing as many of the aspects or points you can think of. You may well rely on your own experience.

You might want to think about the topic from scratch in order to develop your own ideas. You might want to use it to assist you in memorising key points about this topic made in your class notes or in a chapter or section of a textbook that you have just read.

It is often possible to reduce the number of main branches leading from the central focus in the mind map, by making connections and highlighting the most important aspects to obtain an overview. Small drawings and symbols could be used instead of words – they might be more memorable! When selecting these, think about how they might be drawn so that the picture will activate as many of your senses as possible. Use clear, bold colours, perhaps different colours for 'for' and 'against', as they help the overview of the mind map and could improve your recall by 50 per cent or more.

If you prepare a mind map for each topic you have studied, you will have some very useful revision notes. In your final preparation for an examination your mind maps can help enormously, mainly by reminding you of key points and allowing you to concentrate on them straight away.

Review

1 Write MOTOR CAR in the centre of a sheet of plain paper.

Draw curved lines radiating from this central point and at the end of each identify one use or problem. For example, 'transport people' might be one of your uses and 'pollution' one of the problems. Points like this represent the first round of the mapping exercise. Perhaps you could arrange 'uses' on one side and 'problems' on the other.

But then you might ask 'for what reasons are people being transported by car?' Going to work, shopping, visiting and recreation may be among your reasons. Each of these should be represented as a curved line radiating from 'transport people'. Similarly for 'pollution' you might distinguish between different types. Again, each of these second-round points should have its own line radiating from 'pollution'. You might even care to pursue the subject further and come up with some third-round points.

Continue in this way until you think you have exhausted all your relevant ideas. Then check through what you have plotted to see if anything important has been missed (**3.2**). Finally, tidy up or restructure your mind map until you are satisfied with its layout and content.

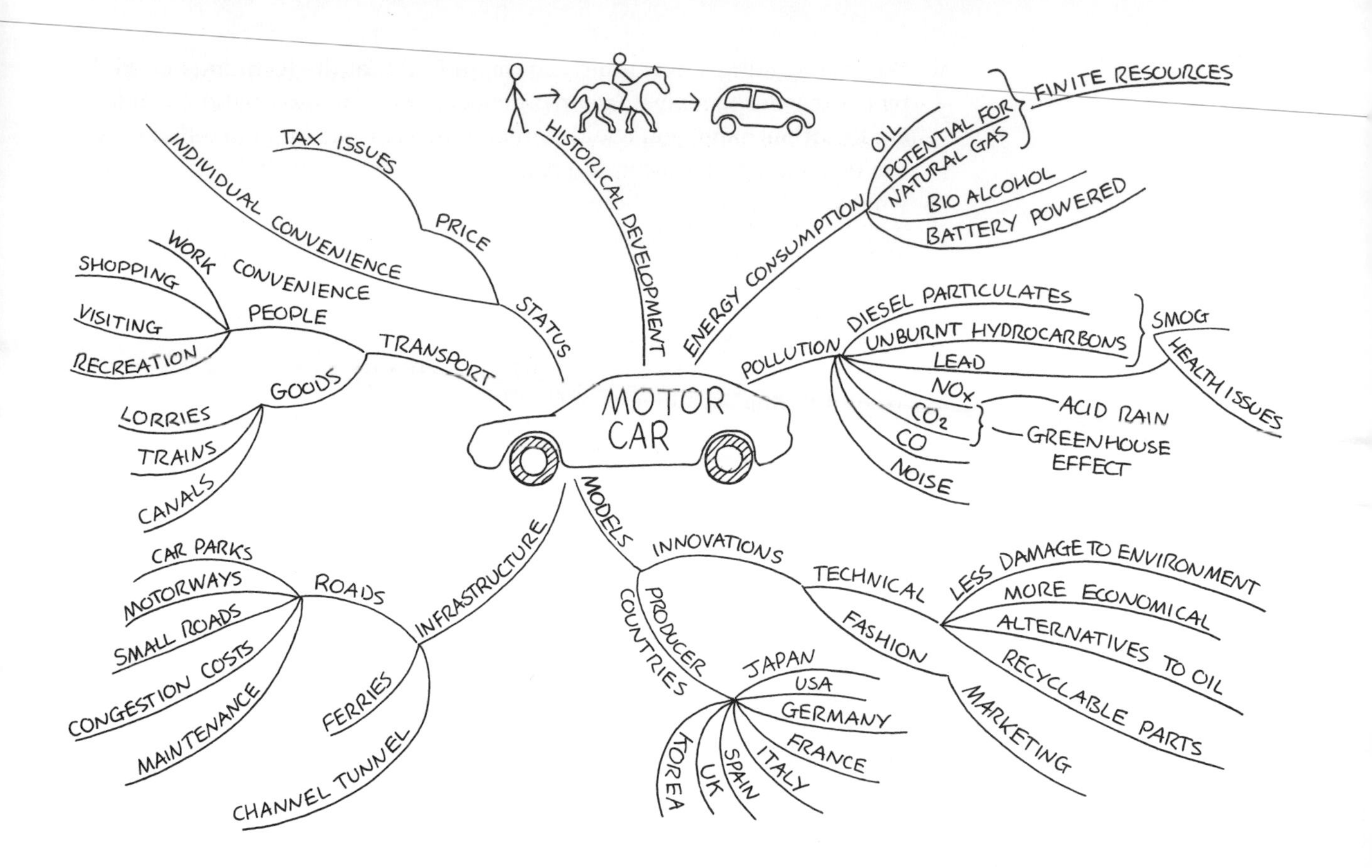

Figure 3.2 A mind map relating to the motor car

Shortcomings of mind mapping

The mind map is a very personal tool which supports the user's own work and efforts. As it is such a personal tool, the technique is not always suitable for group work, but it can work for a common task such as an exercise in planning a group fieldwork project. One of the group should act as a 'scribe' during the brainstorming session, writing up key phrases on a blackboard or flipchart as they occur to members of the group and adding their own if they have ideas to air. The group members might contribute to the work of the whole group by referring to their own mind maps prepared in advance.

The uses of mind maps – an overview

You will find that the mind-map technique is extremely useful in a situation where you are trying to learn new information. As a result of your brainstorming you will find that assimilation and recall of the key ideas becomes relatively easy. Of course, you can use the same technique for organising your ideas when tackling an essay, examination question or even for planning your geographical personal enquiry.

The mind mapping technique can be very useful in a variety of completely different situations. For example:

- When beginning a new topic you might find that the technique is used by the teacher to activate your preconceptions and associations of ideas. On the other hand, you could think about the topic for yourself and use the technique to discover and organise what you already know (or find what you don't know) about the topic.
- As a means of personal preparation for:
  - field visits or investigations
  - experiments or research projects
  - planning essays or answers to exam questions
  - writing up a special study or personal enquiry.
- When revising, as a means of recalling:
  - key points in a lesson, lecture, discussion or tutorial
  - the main points raised in an article or section of a textbook
  - ideas portrayed in films/videos/computer programs.
- Creating ideas for many situations.

SECTION B

Concept mapping

This is slightly different from mind mapping and the technique can be a powerful tool to stimulate clarification of basic concepts. The technique has been successfully used with A-level students, particularly when looking at complex interrelationships, such as we often find in Geography.

Let's start with a practical example. A group of A-level students has spent time working on a project entitled 'The problems of waste disposal'. The group has investigated many aspects of waste disposal by visiting sites in the locality, doing experiments, talking with different people with a special knowledge of the problems and with other local people, seeking their opinions about the 'waste' issue.

As well as group discussion, the teacher has introduced the students to different concepts from the syllabus concerned with the topic, and has also tried to activate the students' recall of concepts that they should have 'learned' earlier in their school careers. However, they may still have difficulty in using these concepts in a meaningful way in their discussion of the waste issue. In other words, the concepts have not yet become an integral part of their 'view of the world'. Instead, when the issue is discussed, they still tend to use common words and ideas rather than the scientific concepts.

Here is an example of how one group developed a concept map. Using their experience and knowledge, they first listed the key concepts concerned with waste disposal. They came up with:

Landfill
Recycling
Re-use
Eutrophication
Greenhouse effect
Incineration
Composting/biogas
Pollution
Sustainable use of resources

Each of these was written on a yellow Post-it® note. Then, using a large sheet of paper, they moved the Post-it® notes around until they were sure they explained how the concepts were linked. To explain the links, they wrote connecting arrows and phrases on the paper until they were satisfied that they had achieved a concept map showing not only how the concepts were linked, but also how other key factors were involved (**3.3**). These other factors, such as soil, biogas and water, they wrote on red Post-it® notes.

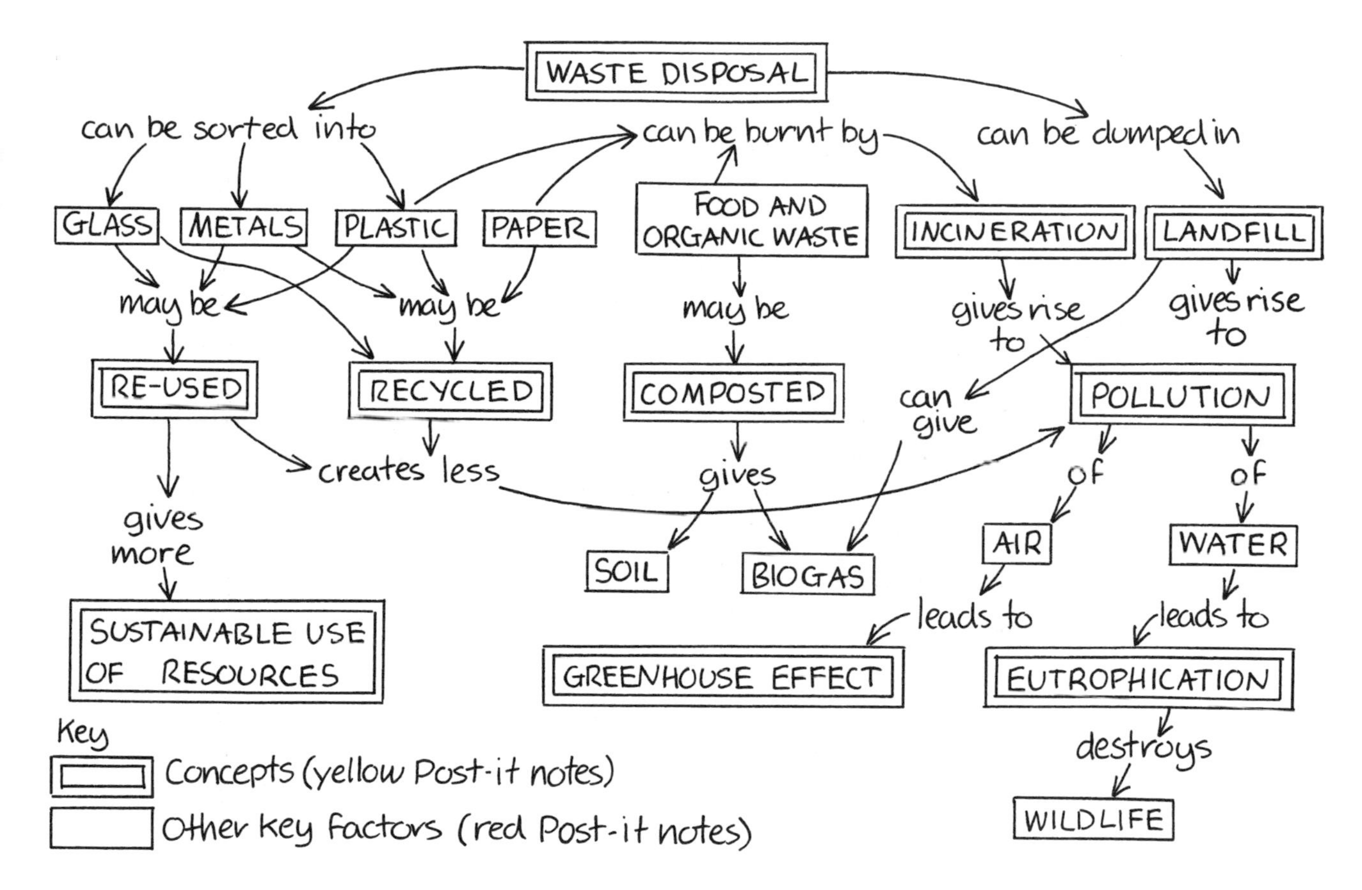

Figure 3.3 A concept map relating to waste disposal

If you use this technique, remember that you may add as many other concepts and connecting words as you wish to create your concept map. The concepts will almost certainly emerge in random order and will need re-arranging into a logical and coherent sequence. Now you can concentrate on improving your understanding of the concepts and the processes involved. You might wish to exchange your concept map with another pair or group, examine its meaning and discuss and share ideas. Discuss all points of disagreement with the whole group.

Concept map **3.4** is an example from another group exploring various issues and concepts associated with the topic of erosion. This time, the concept names were written directly onto a large sheet of paper and frames drawn around each one. Connecting lines were drawn between the concepts, and 'connecting words' added. After a discussion, the group revised their concept map and produced a final version.

The task of concept mapping is stimulating intellectually, provoking

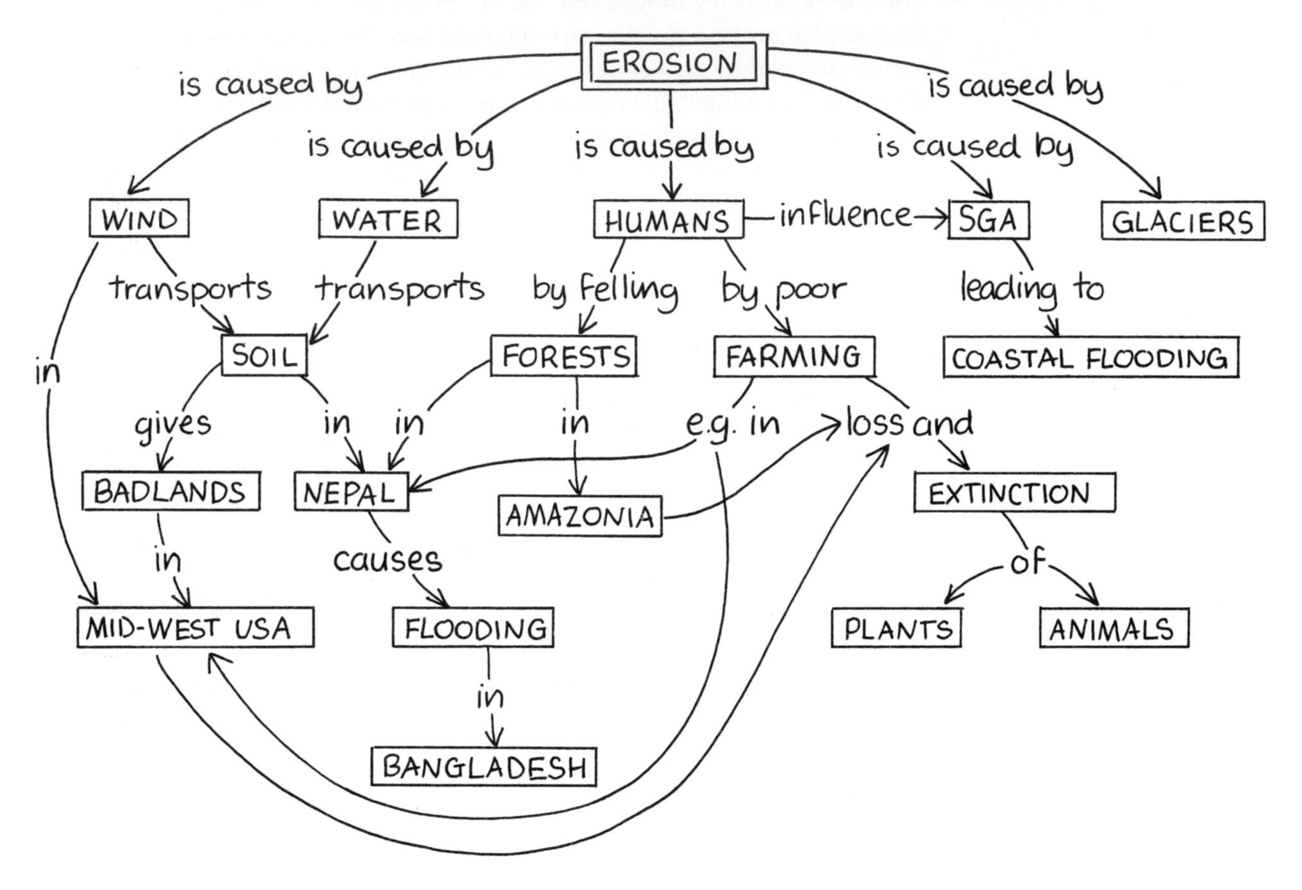

Figure 3.4 A concept map relating to erosion

discussion and creative ideas. Using the technique with a given set of concepts has the advantage of forcing you to concentrate on your understanding of those concepts. In most cases, it is fruitful for you to refer to examples and case studies as you near the end of the chain in your concept map.

You can evaluate your concept maps by asking such questions as:

- Are the connecting words between the specific concepts scientifically meaningful and accurate?
- Is the concept map meaningful and hierarchical from top to bottom?

- Have you done enough work to create meaningful connecting lines in addition to the lines from top to bottom?
- Are good, relevant examples and case studies used?

One thing to watch out for is the apparent close resemblance between concept mapping and mind mapping. Remember that they have different uses. They should be used carefully to add variety to your notes and to help with revision.

Concept-mapping techniques are typically used in regular teaching situations where in general the teacher controls and selects the concepts in focus and the goals to be reached through the learning process. This means that the teacher is able to use the map as a check on how sound the understanding of those concepts really is. Concept maps can be used to summarise sections of class notes, particularly in parts of the subject where there are complex interrelationships.

Mind maps, on the other hand, are a much more personal tool. It is not possible for anyone other than the compiler of the mind map to grasp its full meaning. Mind mapping is much more open-ended than concept mapping and stimulates use of the whole mind. It more fully supports recall, personal experience and creativity as it makes use of pictures and imagination and recognises interactions. It is a highly personal technique which can be used effectively to sort out your ideas on a particular topic.

SECTION C

Pictorial notes

Some people have a very well-developed pictorial memory (a so-called 'photographic memory'). They can remember facts by where they are on the page, for example. We all have some ability in this, but it is much better developed in some people than in others. However, we can all use a trick to make things easier to remember.

First, we have to convert our notes on a particular topic to a sketch of something to do with that topic. For example, if we were studying the tropical forest ecosystem, we might think of a large tree. This can then be used to act as a frame for our notes on the subject. Diagram **3.5** on the next page gives an example of this. You could obviously put as much or as little information on this type of diagram as you like. Try it. If you find that drawing out a shape within which you write the notes helps your recall, then perhaps this method is for you. The tropical forest ecosystem notes here have been written from *Environment and People*, pages 186–88.

Figure 3.5 The tropical rainforest ecosystem

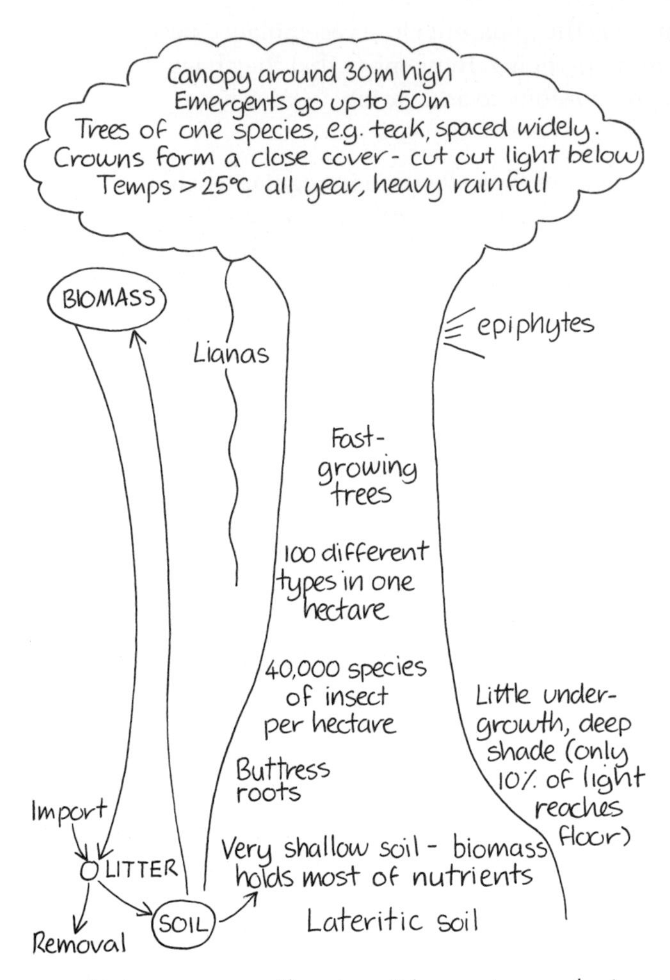

Review

2 Practise the technique by writing similar notes for:

a agricultural change in the South (on a drawing of a large sack)

b the fuelwood crisis in Nepal (on a drawing of a tree with lopped branches)

c the work of waves (on a cross-section drawing of a wave).

You can find details on all of these topics in *Environment and People*, pages 342–44, 362–63 and 50–52 respectively.

You might say that, if you are going to go to the trouble of writing notes as we have just suggested, you may just as well draw a 'proper diagram' and some notes to go with it. That probably means that your mind has been trained to benefit from information presented in a different way, or that you work best with linear information.

Review

3 If you think that is the case, compare your ability to recall information on a subject by seeing how well you do with one topic recalled in the pictorial way and one recalled in the more traditional way.

SECTION D

Fact cards

One more traditional way of learning information that has served many students well is the fact card approach. You can buy commercially produced revision cards in the shops, but many students find that they are dispiriting. The cards often introduce ideas and examples that are new to the students, perhaps even looking at some subjects that are not on their particular syllabus. It is better to make your own.

Review

4 Turn to a section of your coursework notes that you want to learn. Go through it, underlining the most important words. Be fairly ruthless with yourself. You don't want every other word underlined!

Now take a sheet of A4 paper and fold it, lengthways, about a third of the way across. Transfer all your underlined words into the narrower left-hand column. On the right-hand side, write an explanation of the term, a comment or an example. If you were looking at 'Ethnic cleansing in Bosnia' (*Environment and People*, pages 292–94) your notes might start as shown in **3.6**.

Continue with this example, or write your own notes on any part of your course.

Now cover up the left-hand side of the paper and try to remember the words or phrases to which the comments and definitions belong. Or you could try it the other way round: give yourself a test on the meanings or significance of words and terms by covering up the right-hand side.

Bosnia	Part of former Yugoslavia; in 1990 contained Muslims, Serbs, Croats and other minorities.
1989	Communist rule came to an end, in-fighting began.
1992	Bosnia invaded; territory annexed by neighbouring Croatia and Serbia; Muslims displaced.
Ethnic cleansing	The expulsion of 'unwanted' ethnic elements in a population

Figure 3.6 Ethnic cleansing in Bosnia

A refinement of this technique is to transfer the notes not onto an A4 sheet, but to postcards. This ensures that you have taken the trouble to condense your notes, and allows you to carry them round with you so that you can use those 'dead' moments (travelling to school, waiting for a train, etc.), especially those otherwise wasted moments immediately before an exam.

You might like to get together with friends. You could each produce cards, perhaps on different topics, to cut down on the work each of you has to do. You can photocopy the results quite cheaply (or do them on a word processor and print off more than one copy). You would then be in a position to have revision group meetings. Some of the best students I have ever taught have approached it this way – it impresses parents as well!

SECTION E

Mnemonics, word pictures and acronyms

An elaboration on the fact card theme is the use of mnemonics. These are 'pegs' upon which you can hang your memory. For example, we probably all know of the famous rocket scientist Roy G Biv. He it is who, in shooting up through the sky, left a trail behind which showed all the colours of the rainbow: Red, Orange, Yellow, Green, Blue, Indigo, Violet (the letters of his name, in order). Silly, isn't it? However silly it may be, though, I did not have to look before I wrote it. It has stayed with me for over 30 years since I first learned it. The combination of story, picture and initial letters is an extremely potent one for learning.

Mnemonics are often remembered not as names, but as sentences in which the starting letter of the words represents the initial letters of what you want to remember. Thus Roy G Biv could instead have been: Ray often yells 'Great Balls in Vienna!' You can have a bit of fun with these, which helps the learning process no end.

Let's have a look at a more geographical example.

A straight mnemonic would be to take just the initial letters of a list and make a sentence of them. Thus, we might have 'VIP! Sh!' These are the initial letters of the types of eruption – Vesuvian, Icelandic, Peléean, Strombolian and Hawaiian. The mnemonic may be okay for remembering the names, but the order of volcanic force is missing. In other words, there is no helpful picture as we had in the case of Roy G Biv, for example. To make this a more useful example, with the types of eruption in their correct order of force, we end up with the letter sequence I H S V P. Not a very catchy word! What else can we do? Straightforward mnemonics have their limitations.

A very similar device is the acronym. Here the initial letters of a series of words or items make up a word. We have already used one in **Chapter 2** – OWL. There are three more examples in **Chapter 10** (GRADE, SCORE and WASTE). Again, acronyms can be very useful in helping you to remember things.

SECTION F

Word association – remembering lists

Sometimes you see people on television with supposedly super-human memories. They may be blessed with a very good photographic memory, but one thing is for certain. They will have developed 'tricks' to train their minds to remember. One of the best is association. Let's look at this with a real geographical example.

There are five stages in the seral development model (see *Environment and People*, page 177). They are:

- Pioneer stage
- Scrub stage
- Thicket stage
- Mature stage
- Senile stage.

To remember them in order, we can do one of two things.

Association with numbers

The list is in order. So we need to remember 1 = pioneer. I remember a joke about a pioneer. It goes: 'How do you recognise a pioneer?' The answer is: 'He's the one with the arrow in his back.' My mental picture is of a pioneer (a hill-billy type) with a number 1 (an arrow) sticking out of his back. The **pioneer** (to my mind, anyway) is a hill-billy type of character with an animal-skin hat on.

I now think of a dirty number 2 sitting in the bath, **scrub**bing itself.

Then I think of a small wood, a **thicket**, entirely made up of 3s!

My next picture is of a piece of cheese in the shape of a number 4. Someone is opening the fridge door to recoil in horror at the smell given off by this **mature** number 4. Finally, I picture a number 5, using a walking stick, hobbling down the road. It has a long grey beard – it is a **senile** number 5.

Daft, isn't it? But it works. You try it with any ordered list you want to name (preferably, but not necessarily, geographical).

Association in a story

Another way of performing this memory trick is to associate the items on your list in the form of a story. So, for our seral stages, we might first imagine a pioneer sitting in the bath, scrubbing his hands. Next, we would imagine the scrubbing brush growing into a small thicket of scrubbing brushes when he puts it back into the soap dish. As it grows, the thicket starts to smell. It has turned into a mature cheese. Finally the cheese grows a long grey beard. It has become senile.

This is perhaps even sillier than before. It really does not matter, so long as you can remember the stages in order. In fact, it shows the main reason why this sort of trick works. It alerts all your senses and uses them all to perform the memory feat required. You have mental pictures, you can smell the cheese, you can hear the scrubbing, you can touch the brush, and so on. The more you can get all the senses alerted to help you, the better.

So, to return to our volcanic example, how can we learn Icelandic, Hawaiian, Strombolian, Vesuvian and Peléean in the right order, together with some information about each of them? Before we have a go at this, the information we need to capture is shown in **3.7** overleaf.

My favourite method for committing these names and associated facts to memory would be visual linking in the form of a story. I would start by imagining a person, and since we don't know too many Icelanders, I suspect most people think of Björk. Björk appears, gliding in a boat gently out of a split in the rocks. She is wearing a grass skirt (Hawaiian). Her boat is filling up with liquid rock which is coming up through a hole in the centre of the boat. So she grabs a trombone and tries to give a loud blast on it (Strombolian). But the trombone makes a series of small explosions instead of the noise she was expecting. The boat is nearly full of lava now –

Type of eruption	Characteristics
Icelandic	Lava issues gently from fissures.
Hawaiian	There is gentle and regular emission of fluid basalt from a central vent.
Strombolian	Basaltic lava is less fluid; spasmodic escape of gas causes small explosions.
Vesuvian	There are long periods of inactivity during which gas pressure builds up behind the lava that clogs the vent. The blockage is removed by a large explosion or a series of explosions.
Peléean	The violent type of eruption is marked by the *nuée ardente* (a glowing cloud of gas, ash and pumice).

Figure 3.7 Types of volcanic eruption

it has risen to the level of the name of the boat *Vesuvian*. She is getting panic-stricken, so she blows on the trombone very hard indeed. She goes blue in the face and eventually a very large cork is expelled from the instrument together with a very loud noise. This attracts a rescue boat, which arrives with the famous footballer Pelé on board. The two of them embrace and the rescue boat speeds off, not into the setting sun but into a glowing cloud.

Before you dismiss these ideas as crazy or infantile, just try them out on some of your notes. If you approach the process with the positive attitude that you can train your memory, then with a little effort and with help from these tricks, you certainly will improve it.

To sum up, memory tricks can be useful:

- to remember numbered points
- to remember lists, in order
- to remember the details of listed items.

There is no need to use them all the time. They help in the more difficult cases and they are a bit of fun.

Review

5 Look through all the memory tricks described here and decide which you think is best for remembering the volcanic types and their effects. Perhaps you might devise an even more effective one yourself.

SECTION G

Systems diagrams

Some parts of the subject lend themselves to systems diagrams. Perhaps the best-known example is the hydrological cycle. You will have come across this several times in your pre-A-level Geography, so it will be very familiar. It is very familiar to examiners as well, so it could do with a different approach from you to make them take notice.

The traditional hydrological cycle diagram is shown in **3.8a**. In itself, this is easily remembered and can be very useful to you in all sorts of answers.

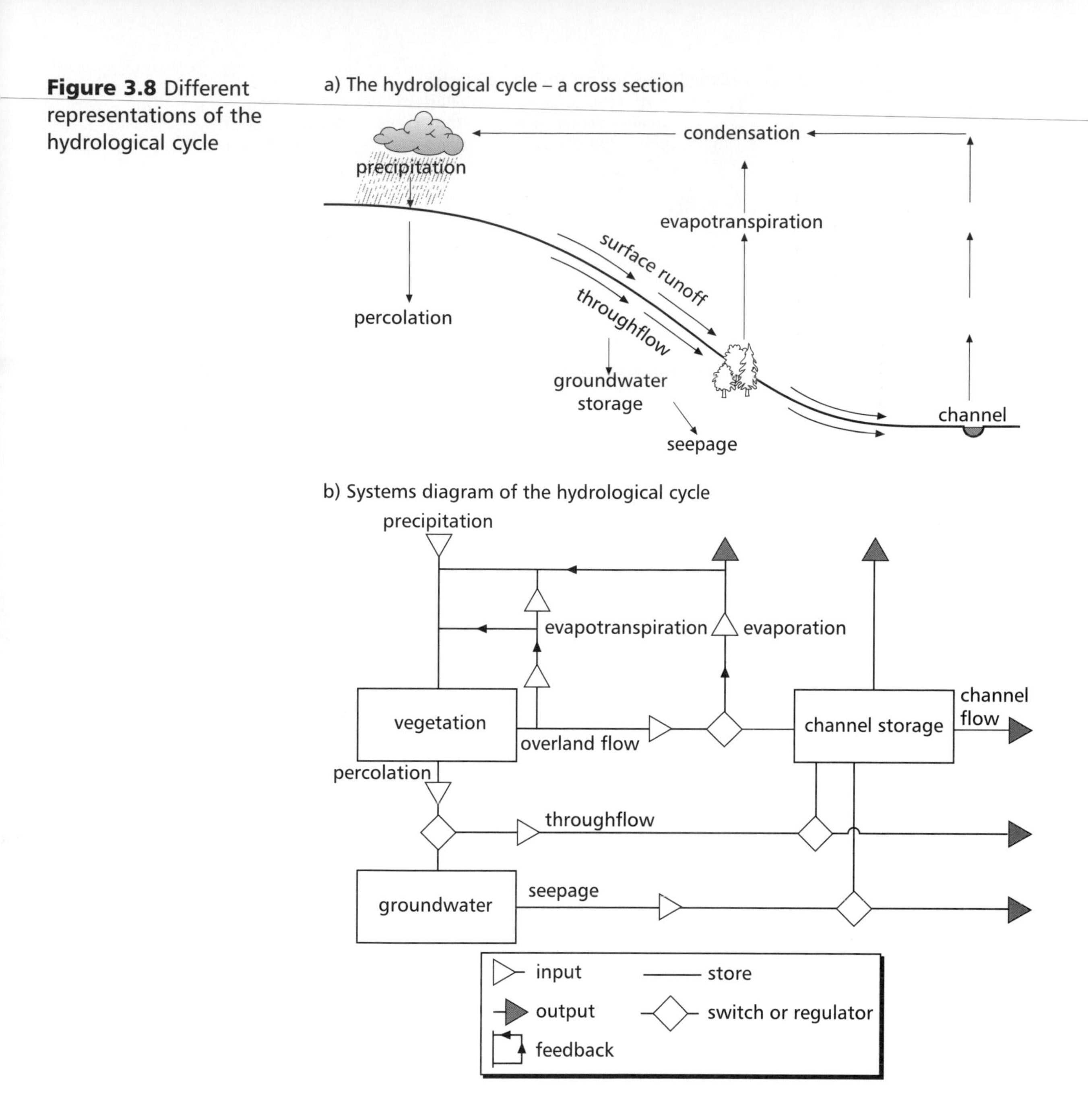

Figure 3.8 Different representations of the hydrological cycle

However, why not make it a bit more scientific and, at the same time, easier to remember? The systems diagram enables you to do this (**3.8b**). There are several symbols associated with drawing these diagrams and they are shown in the key. How about making the systems diagram even more useful? You could do this by relating it to an actual example. For instance, the hydrological cycle is greatly affected in urban areas, where the soil is covered in asphalt, very few trees are left, all the surface rainfall is channelled down drains, and so on.

Figure 3.9 Cross-section of a glacier

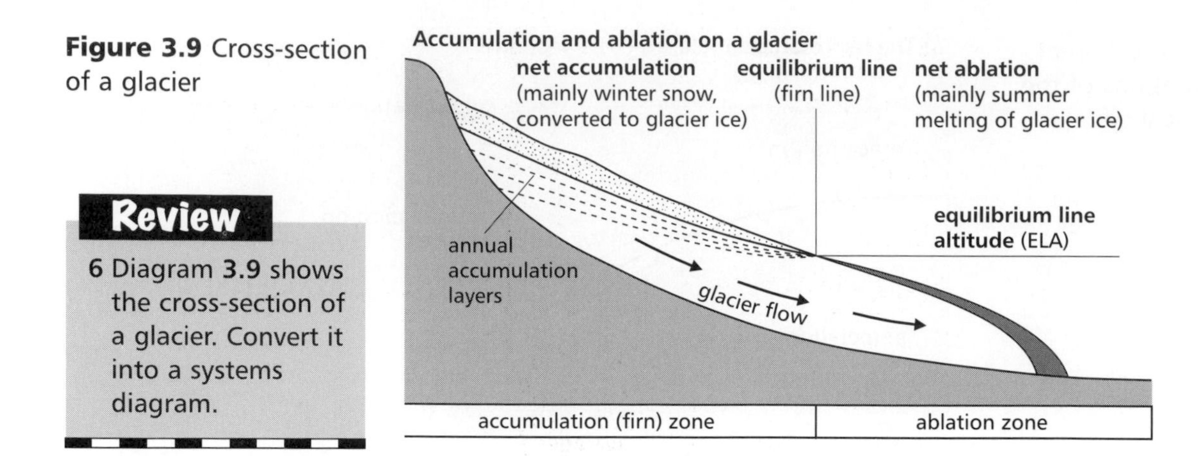

Review

6 Diagram **3.9** shows the cross-section of a glacier. Convert it into a systems diagram.

SECTION H

Remembering the skeleton

If you do not like the idea of memorising lists, or if you have your own favourite way of remembering facts, at least consider remembering the skeleton which you can flesh out in order to present a good, convincing argument.

In any physical geography essay, you will find it easier to ensure that you have said everything necessary if you can remember what headings you have to use. These are like the bones of the skeleton. For example, my list would be as in the box on the left.

FACTORS
Climate
Relief and drainage
Soil
Vegetation
Human interference
Rock type
Rock structure
PROCESSES
Weathering
Erosion
Transport
Deposition
FORM
Each landform type is distinctive

In all physical environments, factors influence processes which in turn help create distinctive landforms. This is shown in **2.3** on page 20. So if we remember the lists of types of factors and processes, we should be able to remember to say something about each one.

Just imagine an essay title: 'Describe and explain how limestone scenery may differ in temperate and tropical areas'. If we are armed with the list of headings we have to use, it suddenly becomes much easier. On the basis that a good, relevant statement earns credit, you can soon clock up the marks this way.

By the way, the list of **factors** and **processes** could be remembered by mnemonics, as by:

Royal **H**arry sometimes **c**orks **r**eally **v**intage **R**ed, **e**ven **w**hen **t**oo **d**runk.

You don't have to remember the factors and processes in any particular order, so they have been re-arranged to make a sentence in this case. What do the letters stand for? Can you invent your own better version?

The same sort of skeleton applies to other areas of Geography as well. For example, if we are studying the location of industry, we might like to remember the main groups of factors that influence it:

Review

7 Write some mnemonics to remember the framework of industrial location factors (**3.10**).

Try to do the same for other major geographical topics.

PHYSICAL FACTORS	COMPETITION
Amount of land Relief Drainage Rock type Climate	Location of other producers
ECONOMIC FACTORS	**GOVERNMENT INTERVENTION**
Distance from market Infrastructure Labour costs Transport costs Economies of scale	Grants Tax incentives Central planning

Figure 3.10 Industrial location factors

SECTION I

Summing up

This chapter has covered a range of different learning techniques. No doubt you were already familiar with some of them, but hopefully you have been introduced to some new ones. All these techniques have certain things in common: they seek to improve your memory power, and as a consequence they raise your ability to absorb, retain and recall factual material. For this reason they are most valuable to you towards the end of the course when effective revision is the order of the day. However, this is not to suggest that you should only bother with them just near examination time. Far from it. They should be an integral part of the notes that you prepare and steadily accumulate throughout the course. Given the diversity of techniques available, it is recommended that you choose those that seem to suit you best. Use them regularly, perhaps refine them, but certainly become proficient in using them. Make them part of your OWL. Do this and you will certainly reap the benefits in the examination room.

CHAPTER

4 Writing essays and answering examination essay questions

In this chapter you will:

- learn about the building blocks of a good essay
- discover ways of making the essay your own
- find encouragement to put your own ideas and personality into your essays.

There are many ways in which you might be tested during the course and in the examinations at the end of it. The one that our student advisors told us was the most difficult for them is the essay and the question demanding an essay-type answer. Some A-level students do not like writing essays. They see it as a chore and often claim they are no good at it. Not only is that a negative attitude that needs to be eliminated, but just think about it for a moment. Can you spot a great opportunity here? If you work on improving your essay skills, you will in the end find yourself pitched against reluctant and under-performing writers. What an opportunity! Why not seize it to make your mark in the seemingly difficult area of essay writing. It will take practice, but this chapter suggests ways of achieving this goal.

Finding your own way to write effective essays is crucial to your success. You will hear a lot of people telling you they 'know' how to write essays and that they must follow a certain pattern to stand any chance of doing well. Whilst it is true that a good essay contains a few well-defined basic elements, it is also true that the best essays, the ones that interest the examiners, are those that show individuality and flair. First, it is necessary to point out the key building blocks of the good essay and suggest techniques you can use to develop your own style.

SECTION A

The building blocks of a good essay

The most important thing to remember is that your essay must have a beginning, a middle and an end. In other words, an introduction, an expansion of your arguments or points, and a conclusion. To a large extent, it is up to you how you tackle each of these elements, but they **must** be there.

The introduction

This might be as brief as one sentence long, but normally covers around a third to a half a side of A4 paper. The sorts of things you might include in it are:

- a definition of terms in the essay title
- quotations from other people (or paraphrases of their arguments to demonstrate their ideas on the subject)
- an idea or viewpoint of your own which you are going to explore in the main body of the essay
- something to 'grab' the examiner's interest.

The expansion

This is a series of paragraphs that develop your argument or discussion points. In certain essays, this might involve presenting different sides of an argument, leading to a conclusion that summarises your considered point of view. Try to work on the basis that each paragraph should contain one developed idea.

You should try to avoid writing a purely factual essay. The examiner will be more impressed if you show that you have thought about the subject and that you can discuss ideas as well as recall facts. Even in the very straightforward essays that describe the development of certain landscape features, for example, you could show individuality by using examples local to you, or putting the landscape into context by commenting on its potential for tourism or other economic activity.

The conclusion

This is **not** simply a repetition of some of the points you have already made. That would be a 'summary'. It is a considered, balanced conclusion that either reiterates your view based on the evidence you have presented or builds on the facts you have given in some other way. It might very well refer back to your introduction and should certainly refer to the question itself.

So how do we put this model into practice?

SECTION B

The essay plan

Do not expect to find this easy at first. It is a valuable skill that is developed by hard work. Very few people are natural essay writers, so you have as good a chance as anyone if you are prepared to work at developing your competence. You should also be prepared to make a few mistakes on the way, but do not get disheartened. With practice, you can do it. You should realise that coursework essays are an ideal opportunity to practise your skills, not a punishment for having chosen to study geography. They are there to help and will do so if you view them positively.

The first step to producing a good essay is to write a good plan. When you make your early attempts at writing essays, you should aim to produce plans covering about one side of A4 paper. Later, you will be able to be much briefer than this, but more detail is preferable to begin with, until you have got the hang of it.

Always use the three headings ('Introduction', 'Expansion' and 'Conclusion') in planning your essay. There can be any number of ways of writing each one. So don't think that because everyone should be structuring their writing that way, it might be nice to try something else.

Next, decide on your argument. If the essay title is a statement, you might decide to give evidence for and against it, coming up with your own conclusion (supported, of course, by actual examples). An example might be:

> *'Landforms in hot deserts are as much the result of past as they are of present processes.' Discuss.*

Introduction

When you have decided on your theme, think about how you can introduce it:

- to set the scene for your argument
- to provide a stimulating and exciting opening
- to introduce and define any important terms.

In the case of this question, a plan of the introduction might look like this:

- Understanding of processes very important to true understanding of landscape. Example of Tom Mix and crew, drowned in Death Valley.
- Hot deserts found in tropical and subtropical areas where daytime temperatures often reach 35°C and annual precipitation totals less than 25mm.
- All landscapes develop over time and show evidence of climatic change – hot deserts no exception.

This plan might translate into the following complete version when you write the essay:

> *Tom Mix, a silent-film star, was camping with his film crew on location in a wadi in the Californian Desert (Death Valley) when he was caught in a sudden flash flood and drowned. These people displayed a lack of understanding of the processes that operate in this environment and they paid with their lives. Death Valley is an example of a hot desert. It has developed in the rainshadow of the Sierra Nevada mountains. In such areas, the daytime temperature can reach to over 35°C and rocks become too hot to touch. The annual precipitation is less than 250mm and some places, in the Atacama Desert of Chile for example, have not seen any rain for over 200 years. So if there is so little water in the environment today, how was there a valley such as that in which Tom Mix drowned?*

This introduction hopefully interests you/the reader, slips in a definition, and sets the scene for the argument that the landscape owes at least something to processes no longer operating.

Expansion

Step 1 Evidence for water activity in deserts:
- wadis
- alluvial fans
- dry lake beds (salt pans)
- human, animal and plant remains

Step 2 Evidence for a relationship between present processes and landforms:
- weathering
- deflation hollows
- rock pedestals and other undercut features
- dunes

Step 3 Present water activity – powerful enough to form the features discussed?

This plan illustrates several important points. It avoids 'the list'. The list is the death of the good essay. If ever you find yourself saying 'firstly', 'secondly', 'thirdly', etc. in an essay, think again. You are falling into the trap of trying to mention everything you have learned about a subject rather than trying to answer the question set. You should be trying to find the **best** examples to illustrate your argument. For instance, Step 2 requires examples of:

- desert weathering (granular disintegration)
- wind erosion (deflation)
- wind transport (and its effect as shown by rock pedestals)
- wind deposition (dunes).

It avoids listing all the different types of erosion and deposition. A good 30 per cent of the candidates will probably do just this, in the mistaken belief that the essay has to include every known feature of a hot desert landscape. No doubt some of them will, for good measure, even throw in a few fanciful ones only ever spotted once in the depths of the Iranian Desert!

The plan **builds up the argument**. Step 1 gives evidence of water activity in deserts (some present, some past). Step 2 gives evidence for a direct relationship between current processes and landforms. Step 3 discusses whether all the surface features in today's hot deserts could have been formed by the processes currently operating, especially the action of water.

One thing we have not yet mentioned is the **use of examples** (see **Chapter 5**). For each of the processes or features named, either a case study should be used (within which they can be located) or actual examples should be quoted. This crucially makes the answer a geographical rather than a geological one.

This three-step expansion leads therefore to a natural conclusion, a plan for which follows.

Conclusion

Partly agree. Some landforms very closely related to present processes, especially wind deposition. Some show more evidence of past processes. Statement is a generalisation. All hot deserts are a palimpsest [see below], *relating to climatic fluctuation over geological time. Some reflect past processes more than others.*

This is often a line that you can take in 'discuss' essays. Their titles are often generalisations that you can challenge. In this case, you can modify the statement. In other cases, you may agree, disagree or suggest a compromise. The full version of our plan for the conclusion might be:

It is untrue to say that all hot desert landscapes exhibit as much relation to past climatic conditions as to present ones. Some, as in the case of the ergs of the Central Sahara, are almost entirely related to granular disintegration, deflation and wind deposition under present conditions. The extent of desert weathering, erosion, transportation and deposition may even be greater now, for instance in those areas suffering 'desertification'. This is the magnification of desert processes, often due to human activity. Other areas, such as Death Valley, where Tom Mix died, reflect water-cut features created in a previous (pluvial) environment and are now being maintained by the occasional flash flood. Yet others fall between these two extremes. Hot deserts are not unique in this. They show the results of climatic fluctuation over geological time just as clearly as do glacial or temperate landscapes. All landscapes are a ***palimpsest****, showing layers of different influences in their formation. There is evidence for the operation of past processes in all hot desert landscapes, but to say that past processes have a bearing equal to that of present ones is too much of a generalisation.*

The word **palimpsest** is a useful one for a geographer. It refers to any document that has been changed by successive users. To an original map, for example, have been added new roads, houses and factories. The result, a palimpsest, is one document, but it reflects many stages of addition and usage. Landscape development is just like that.

Review

Get hold of sets of previous examination papers related to the particular syllabus you are studying.

1 Establish which paper or papers require you to write essay answers.

2 Practise writing plans for some of those answers, first at your leisure and then, as you become more confident, against the clock.

3 Compare your plans with those produced by some of your friends. You will be surprised how much you learn!

SECTION C

Condensing the plan

It is good practice in examinations to write out your plan in pencil on the answer paper itself. Once you have followed it to write your essay, you may cross it out with one diagonal stroke. The examiner can therefore still read it and is duty-bound to give you credit, even if you run short of time or for any reason do not finish the essay. You would not, by this stage, be writing a plan of the length we have just considered. By now, you will be writing a condensed version. This might appear as follows.

Intro.
Hot desert landscapes = present & past processes. Day 35°C, annual ppt under 250mm. Atacama even drier.
Exp.
1 Water in deserts
weathering (basal undercutting)
erosion (wadis)
deposition (fans)
human, animal and plant remains
2 Present conditions
weathering (granular disintegration)
transport (wind, forming rock pedestals)
erosion (deflation)
deposition (dunes)
3 Balance of past v present.
Conc.
Generalisation – more true in some areas than others. Desertification.

It might take you three minutes to write out a plan like this, once you have practised the technique. It would be three minutes very well spent, because it will ensure that you stick to the question being asked. The logical progression guarantees a well-developed argument. An improvement would be to indicate where you might add sketches or diagrams, which we will deal with in **Chapter 6**.

SECTION D

Writing the essay

Armed with your plan and bearing the question in mind at all times, you should then write the essay. Do not expect to be writing flat-out at all times. A well-planned essay will give you time to think and check you from trying to include everything you ever learned about the topic. It will select the best pieces of information and use them to produce a really good answer.

Timing is crucial. In the examination, work out how much time you have for each answer and do not exceed it. Bear in mind that you need time to calmly read through the paper (certainly more than once) and to carefully select those questions that are best for you (two vital aspects of good examination technique – see **Chapter 10**). Keep an eye on the clock, but do not panic yourself. If you plan properly, you should have plenty of time to complete your essay. Practice makes perfect. Teachers are usually delighted to mark any 'extra' work that you undertake by yourself. Indeed, completing such work really should be regarded as 'essential' practice.

The essay should always include plenty of evidence to support your argument. In Geography, that evidence comes from examples and case studies. The next two chapters explain how you can master them to make your essay answers even better.

The use of such illustrative supporting material is certainly one way of 'personalising' your work. Another is your style of writing. The bottom line here is clarity of communication. Express yourself clearly and concisely and you will get your ideas and arguments across. There is nothing more off-putting to an examiner than muddled and muddied writing. Getting your knowledge and understanding across is best achieved by writing simple sentences. A sound use of vocabulary will also help – this will include an appropriate use of technical terms. In addition, you might try to get something of the vitality of speech into your writing. In doing so, however, there is a risk of straying from strictly grammatical English. Your vocabulary may also become rather colloquial. So don't go over the top! What do you think of the following sentence taken from a student essay on the central business district?

> *In the 1960s trendy architects and town planners often bulldozed old town centres and put up naff concrete piles, many of them being demolished since.*

We know what is meant and it is certainly not long-winded, but ...!

Now plan an essay to answer the following question:

> *'The risk of flooding has often been increased by the development of drainage basins.' Using detailed examples, explain why this has happened and what can be done about it.*

Try planning your own answer first, but here is one student's condensed plan.

Intro.	Flooding is a natural process – recurrence intervals. Due to combination of factors, but if factors are affected, for instance by development, the recurrence interval can be greatly reduced.
Step 1	Theory – draw two cross-sections to show how the natural hydrological cycle for the Thames valley has been affected by farming and building near Maidenhead.
Step 2	Detailed example – Chichester, 1996–97.
Step 3	Remedial action – flood relief channel at Chichester.
Step 4	Other examples – sketch map to show possible methods: avoid building on floodplain, improve drainage, plant water-loving trees (willow, etc.), manage the channel (levées, sluice gates, flood basins, etc.).
Conc.	Floods are more frequent in some drainage basins – due to mismanagement or perhaps rainfall change or even mismanagement upstream. Particularly important when floods downstream result from exploitation upstream in a different country (e.g. Ganges – deforestation in Nepal and India, floods in Bangladesh). Show importance of integral drainage basin management.

SECTION E

How essays are marked

You might be interested to have some insight into how essay answers are marked by the examination boards. It is not possible to generalise for all boards, but in general essay answers are marked out of 25. Marks are awarded under three headings of knowledge, understanding, and skills. Under each of the headings, three or more broad levels of attainment may be defined. The following scheme used by one examination board should give you some flavour of assessment criteria.

Knowledge of relevant concepts, issues and case studies	
Marks	**Mark band descriptor**
8–7	Sound knowledge of case studies, concepts and issues. Relevant and detailed case study information showing sound locational knowledge
6–4	Satisfactory knowledge of case studies, issues and concepts. May lack detail and depth and stray in terms of relevance.
3–1	Generalised knowledge and lacking reference to specific case studies. Knowledge of concepts insecure and uncertain. Considerable irrelevance.

Continues overleaf

Understanding of relevant issues and concepts and their application	
Marks	**Mark band descriptor**
10–7	Sound understanding of the key issue(s), concepts, and case studies, well applied and highly relevant to the question. Evidence of evaluative comment.
6–4	Satisfactory understanding with some application of relevant case study material. Less evidence of an ability to evaluate. At the lower end tends to be descriptive rather than analytical or evaluative.
3–1	Weak grasp of concepts, issues and relevant case study material. Description only.

Skills	
Marks	**Mark band descriptor**
7–6	Good use of language, including appropriate geographical terminology. Coherent arguments showing clear evidence of planning and a logical approach. Possible use of relevant sketch maps and diagrams. Clarity of expression with high standard of accuracy in grammar, spelling and punctuation.
5–4	Reasonable clarity and fluency of expression with some use of appropriate geographical terminology. Arguments are generally relevant with some evidence of planning and structure. Some illustrative material. Grammar, spelling and punctuation largely satisfactory.
3–1	Basic ideas put across but not always in a logical structure. Limited use of appropriate terminology. Scant evidence of planning and trying to argue a case. English is basic and at times faulty.

SECTION F

Summing up

When writing an essay try to consider the following tips:

- Always plan your essay.
- Stick to that plan and frequently refer back to the title or question as a check.
- Structure your essay into three parts – an introduction, expansion and conclusion.
- Don't think that you have to write down everything that you have ever learned about a particular topic.
- Avoid simply writing lists.
- Description is no substitute for analysis, evaluation and argument.
- Use examples and case studies wherever possible and don't be frightened to express your own ideas.
- Write simply and clearly, and remain relevant.

CHAPTER

5 Supporting your work with case studies

SECTION A

Introduction

An A-level Chief Examiner recently wrote:

> *Geography is all about places and therefore it is quite amazing to read so many examination answers that manage to avoid referring to anywhere on the Earth's surface! Such essays often do incorporate models and theories into their analysis, but these alone give a very incomplete view of geography. Our subject is a spatial one and above all very dynamic. Consequently, models and theories rarely stand the test of time for very long. Case studies tell it like it is.*

In this chapter you will learn:

- how to find good case studies
- how to prepare them for examination purposes
- how to use them well, particularly in essay answers.

You will be able to find many detailed case studies in the geography textbooks and magazines. For example, in *Environment and People*, they are shown in yellow-tinted boxes to separate them from the main text and to make them easy for you to use.

Most A-level Geography syllabuses stress the use of case studies or specific examples that focus on a located and defined area. A case study can be used to illustrate a range of geographical features and ideas, such as different types of physical landscape, the relationships between people and their physical surroundings, an environmental problem or issue or any aspect of human geography. The proper use of a case study makes it easier to understand complex issues and relationships. It also provides a specific example from which more general observations or principles may be drawn.

Since 1995, all A-level Geography syllabuses have had to examine what is called the **Common Core**. You will find details of this in the syllabus description published by your GCE Examination Board. In most cases, you will find references to required case studies. Depending on your particular syllabus, it might be a study of two large urban areas (one in the developing world and the other in the developed world) or a study of a large river basin and the physical processes operating in it. In addition to those that may be specified in the syllabus, you might add more to build up a list of some 10 case studies that cover the Common Core. You then need to learn facts, figures and if possible a map or diagram so that you are ready to adapt the case studies for the various ways in which they may be used to exemplify points you are making.

Very often examination questions require you to illustrate your answer with reference to detailed examples or case studies. It is no good saying 'In the developing world today there is much rural–urban migration, e.g. in Africa'! It is certainly the case that examples relevant to the question do occur in Africa, but it is a huge continent and you must be very specific in your location and include appropriate diagrams and sketch maps if possible. So what makes a good case study and how do you find and prepare them for your use, particularly in examinations?

SECTION B

Finding good case studies

Keeping up with events

Modern Geography is principally about the real world of today. You need to be aware of important changes taking place in our environment and society. The horrendous events occurring in the African Sahel over the last few decades are a classic example of the sort of contemporary issue that the A-level Geography student should know about. You should understand that the problems of the Sahel are the outcome of interactions between dynamic environmental and human systems. Similar examples are happening all the time. As I write, south-east Asia is covered in a smoke-haze from fires burning out of control in Sumatra, and the island of Montserrat is being threatened by a volcanic eruption. These are exactly the sort of current event I would include in my case-study notes, and again the two key aspects would be causes and consequences.

One of the things that distinguishes A-level study is being left more to your own devices than at GCSE. You will be expected to gain some of the knowledge and understanding required by the syllabus through independent work outside the classroom. A significant dimension of this self-study in Geography should also involve the collection of appropriate and preferably up-to-date case studies to reinforce and illustrate your work. Such material can be found in a variety of ways:

- constant referencing to at least one modern A-level textbook (case studies are often boxed off to help you home in on them)
- reading a range of appropriate geographical magazines and journals (e.g. *Geography Review*, *Geographical Magazine*, *GeoFile*, etc.)
- your own fieldwork – this can be a particularly good source of case-study material and you should easily remember the detail
- reading a daily broadsheet newspaper (e.g. *The Guardian*, *Independent* or *Times*)
- watching the news and relevant documentary programmes on television
- searching the Internet.

One of best ways today of keeping up to date and the best source of case-study material is the last – the Internet. There is a whole range of web sites giving details of recent volcanic activity, glacial work, planning enquiries and so on. Hopefully, your teachers are encouraging you to use this wonderful information highway.

So there's really no excuse for not keeping up to date with contemporary affairs – there are plenty of sources that are accessible to you. The great bonus of following current events is that you will automatically collect plenty of case-study material. That, in turn, will enrich your geographical studies.

The local area

It is true to say that some of the best and freshest case studies are those derived from a student's own experiences. Many of these experiences will relate to the home area. You can hardly avoid observing and interpreting changes that are occurring in your local environment whether it is urban or rural. Some of these changes, such as the growth in organic farming practices or the proposed route for a local by-pass, may well develop into something of a local issue. You will inevitably hold some views and develop certain attitudes with regard to these developments. Your local area therefore represents a rich source of case-study material that you can tap into. Do not be afraid to express your personal views or values regarding any such issue. Such an approach will tell the examiner a lot about you as a 'thinking' geographer.

Many of you will also make use of some aspect of your local geography for the personal fieldwork investigation that is required by all A-level Geography syllabuses (see **Chapter 9**). As a result of the collection of first-hand or primary data and also by using secondary sources, you will quickly become quite knowledgeable about a particular aspect of your local environment. If you are lucky, you may have the opportunity to display this knowledge and understanding when you are answering an examination question. In short, if your local knowledge is relevant, then do cash in on it in your essays and answers. Remember also that your local newspaper can often be a good source of suitable material.

Review

1 Make a list of geographical examples drawn from your local area about which you know enough detail to be able to use them in examination answers.

If you do not know enough, at least start identifying possibilities. How about the nearest town – could you draw a sketch map of its spatial structure? Has the local river undergone any modifications lately; if so, why? What about recent changes in local farming or the countryside? The list is endless.

Collecting case studies

You need to be very disciplined in your collection of case studies. It is quite easy to accumulate an overwhelming number of them and to drown in a mass of information. You should constantly review what you have collected and not be frightened to jettison material. The key questions to ask all the time are:

- What syllabus topic might this particular case study support?
- Do I already have a case study for this topic?
- Does this new case study illustrate the same point or a different one? If the former is the case, then discard whichever one you think is the weaker.
- Does this topic need case studies at different spatial scales? If so, what scales would be appropriate – local, regional, national or global?
- Which topics still need supporting case studies?

Effective case-study collection certainly needs you to be highly selective. It also requires that you try to keep what you have got as up to date as possible. You might find it useful to collect your case studies in a logbook and organised according to the main syllabus themes or topics. For example, one of your topics might be 'Natural hazards'. In this case, it would be a sensible idea to keep a record of any natural disasters that occur during your course. You will need to note the key details of each event, not just the names and dates, and perhaps insert any newspaper articles or cuttings you come across. It will certainly impress the examiner if you are able to recall relevant, recent examples. It will make it clear that you think geography is about the real world of today and not simply a collection of ideas gleaned from textbooks. An example will show what we mean.

Let us assume that the exam question asks you to refer to an example of a river that is managed in order to provide some degree of flood control. You will not score many marks if you simply refer to 'the Mississippi' or 'the Colorado'. What the examiner is looking for is evidence of your understanding of the principles of river management. Thus, if the Mississippi is your preferred example, you should refer to:

- the storage of potential flood water in reservoirs along such tributaries as the Tennessee and Missouri
- the creation of 'safe' flood overspill areas along its course
- channel straightening
- the construction of levées – there are some 3000km of these up to 15m high built along the course of the river and its chief tributaries.

You might also refer to the fact that, in spite of the completion of various flood control measures, the Mississippi still floods in exceptional circumstances and, indeed, the risk of severe damage may have actually increased if the measures fail. From your log, you would also recall that in August 1993, after a very wet year and having received exceptional rainfall over two times greater than normal for the time of year, the Mississippi burst its banks. Forty-five people were killed as it inundated its floodplain through nine states from North Dakota to Missouri. These recent details will certainly have raised even more the value of your Mississippi case study.

Keeping a log of up-to-date detail on carefully selected case studies and examples is clearly a good investment of time and effort. Hopefully, you will reap the benefits in your essays and examination answers. The competent use of case studies is the main thing that separates a good A-level student from an 'also ran'. Below are a few tips to ensure that you are one of the best.

SECTION D

Preparing a case study

Let us assume that you are studying the causes and consequences of population movement and that you have collected information about population change in the British countryside as your main example of rural–urban migration. Your notes are set out like those shown in **5.1** (from *Environment and People*, page 295).

First of all, you will need to get the information into a form that you will be able to remember and use in a variety of ways. This will require simplifying the map of England and Wales in your notes (perhaps a photocopy given to you by your teacher). It is a complex one. You need to make it work for you in the context of an essay.

You will not be able to recall the whole map in examination conditions. So we need in some way to reduce and simplify the descriptive element or basic messages of the map. The annotated map **5.2** on page 51 shows one possible solution. Note that there is no explanation on this map; it simply describes the **pattern**.

We now need to integrate the text and the map to explain **why** this pattern has come about. This could be solved by producing a series of bullet-point notes to go with **5.2** or another annotated sketch map (**5.3**, page 51).

The two maps together have now captured all the key information in the case study, minus the piece about Tips End. This could be simplified as indicated in **5.4** on page 52.

Note that we have no idea what Tips End looks like. The diagram **5.4** is not a map, but a model to show the changes between the two dates. Its shape does not matter in this context.

CASE STUDY

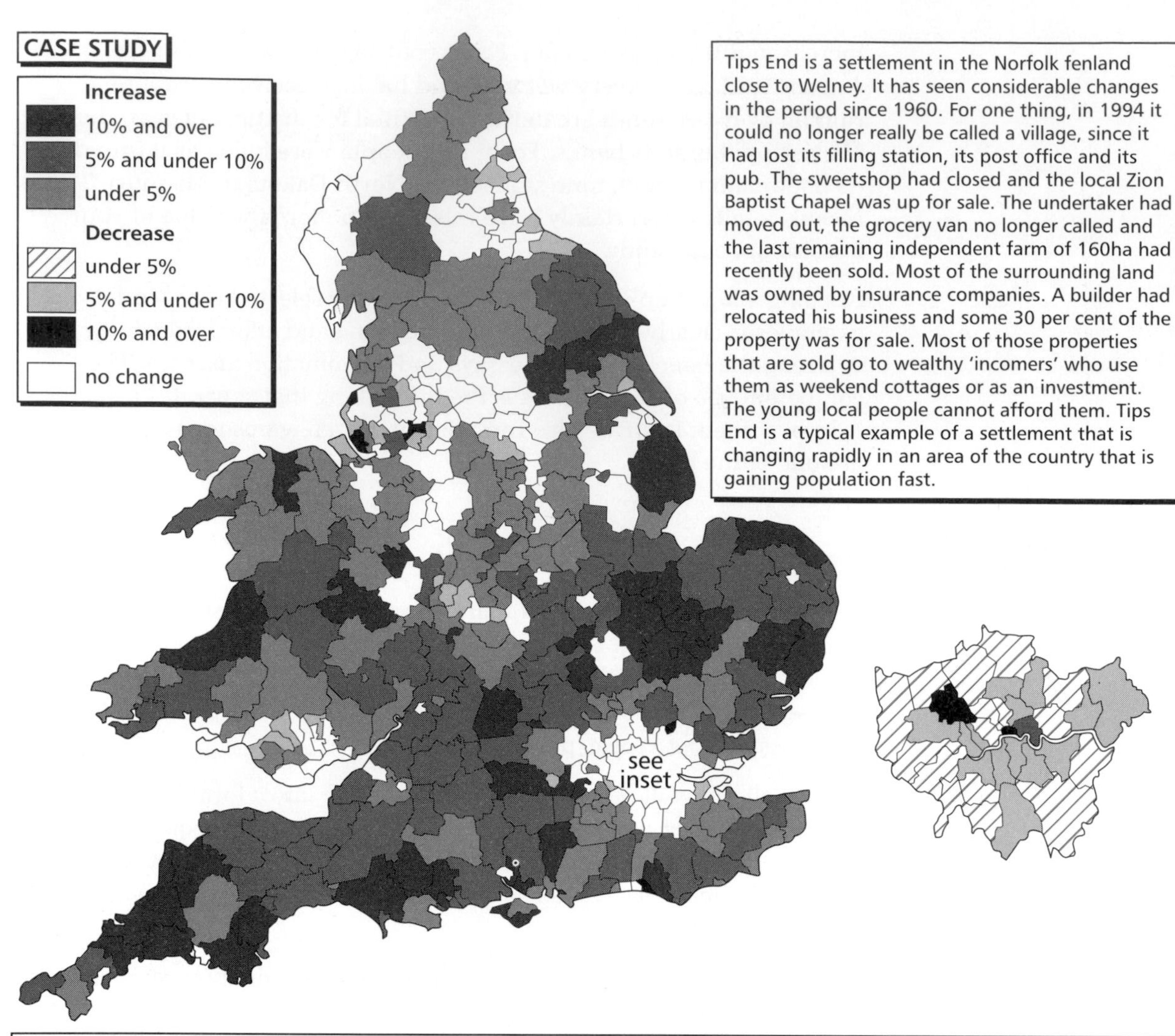

Tips End is a settlement in the Norfolk fenland close to Welney. It has seen considerable changes in the period since 1960. For one thing, in 1994 it could no longer really be called a village, since it had lost its filling station, its post office and its pub. The sweetshop had closed and the local Zion Baptist Chapel was up for sale. The undertaker had moved out, the grocery van no longer called and the last remaining independent farm of 160ha had recently been sold. Most of the surrounding land was owned by insurance companies. A builder had relocated his business and some 30 per cent of the property was for sale. Most of those properties that are sold go to wealthy 'incomers' who use them as weekend cottages or as an investment. The young local people cannot afford them. Tips End is a typical example of a settlement that is changing rapidly in an area of the country that is gaining population fast.

Population change in the British countryside

More than 80 per cent of Britain is rural, but only 20 per cent of the population lives and works in the countryside. Villages and hamlets all over the country, in the Fenlands of East Anglia, the hills of mid-Wales and the Downs of Sussex, for example, are losing their 'local' inhabitants as 'outsiders' move in. The agriculturally-based work opportunities are declining as farms become even larger and more mechanised. Local housing becomes too expensive for local people and is bought up by commuters or by people using it for weekend accommodation (i.e. second homes). The demand for local services, such as the shop and the post office, declines and they close down. People have to travel many miles to shop, and living in the countryside becomes more and more expensive as a result.

The results of the 1991 census showed considerable locational changes for the population as a whole. The map is of districts of England and Wales showing the change in population in the period 1981–91. In general, it shows large increases in some of the more 'rural' areas as people relocate from the cities, but it also highlights some rural areas that are losing population heavily.

Some of the reasons for moving into rural areas are the following:

- *Retirement.* People who have served all their working days in the rush and bustle of urban surroundings move to the quiet of rural areas, often in coastal areas or where they had previous family links.
- *To find a better 'quality of life'.* Some people move to smallholdings or to run rural businesses well before retirement age because it offers them a more relaxed, more rewarding way of life.
- *To run their business from a remote location.* With the availability of efficient fax, telephone and computer links, there is little to keep urban commuters from carrying out many of their tasks from a rural location. This is called 'teleworking' or 'telecommuting'.
- *Relocation of businesses.* Apart from individuals moving to rural locations, whole businesses are doing the same. Some have relocated to such areas as mid-Wales and the southern Lake District, to areas which are not only much more scenically acceptable to the workforce but which also offer financial incentives for moves (such as heavy subsidies for industrial units).

Figure 5.1 Population change in the British countryside

Figure 5.2 A sketch map to show recent population trends in south-east England, 1981–91

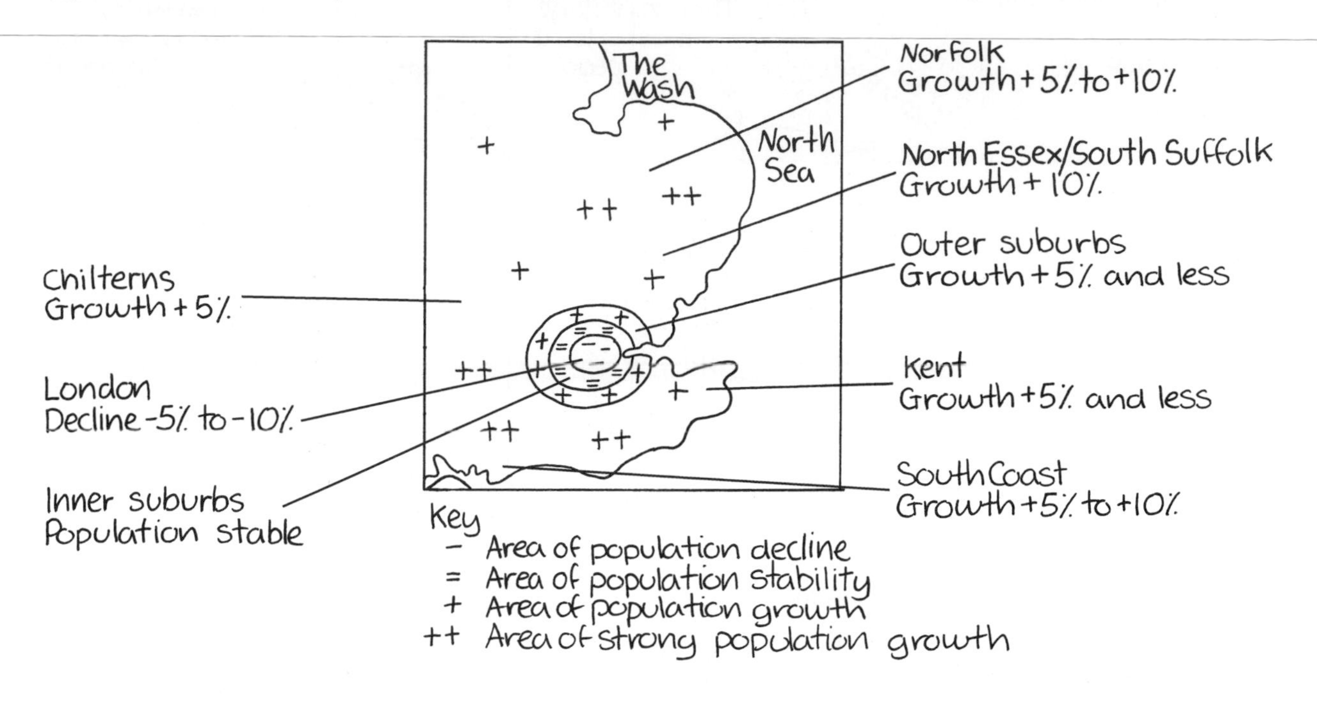

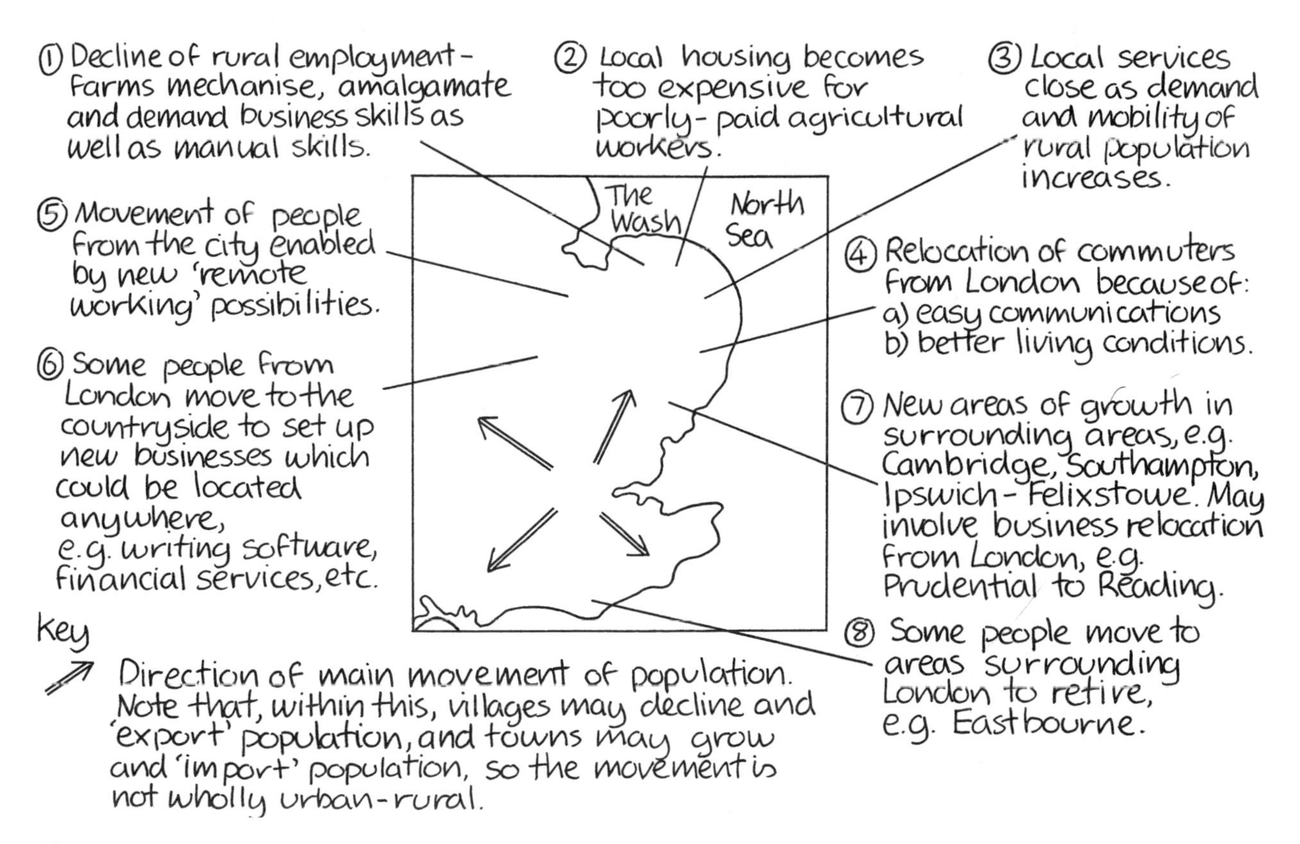

Figure 5.3 An explanation of recent population trends in south-east England, 1981–91

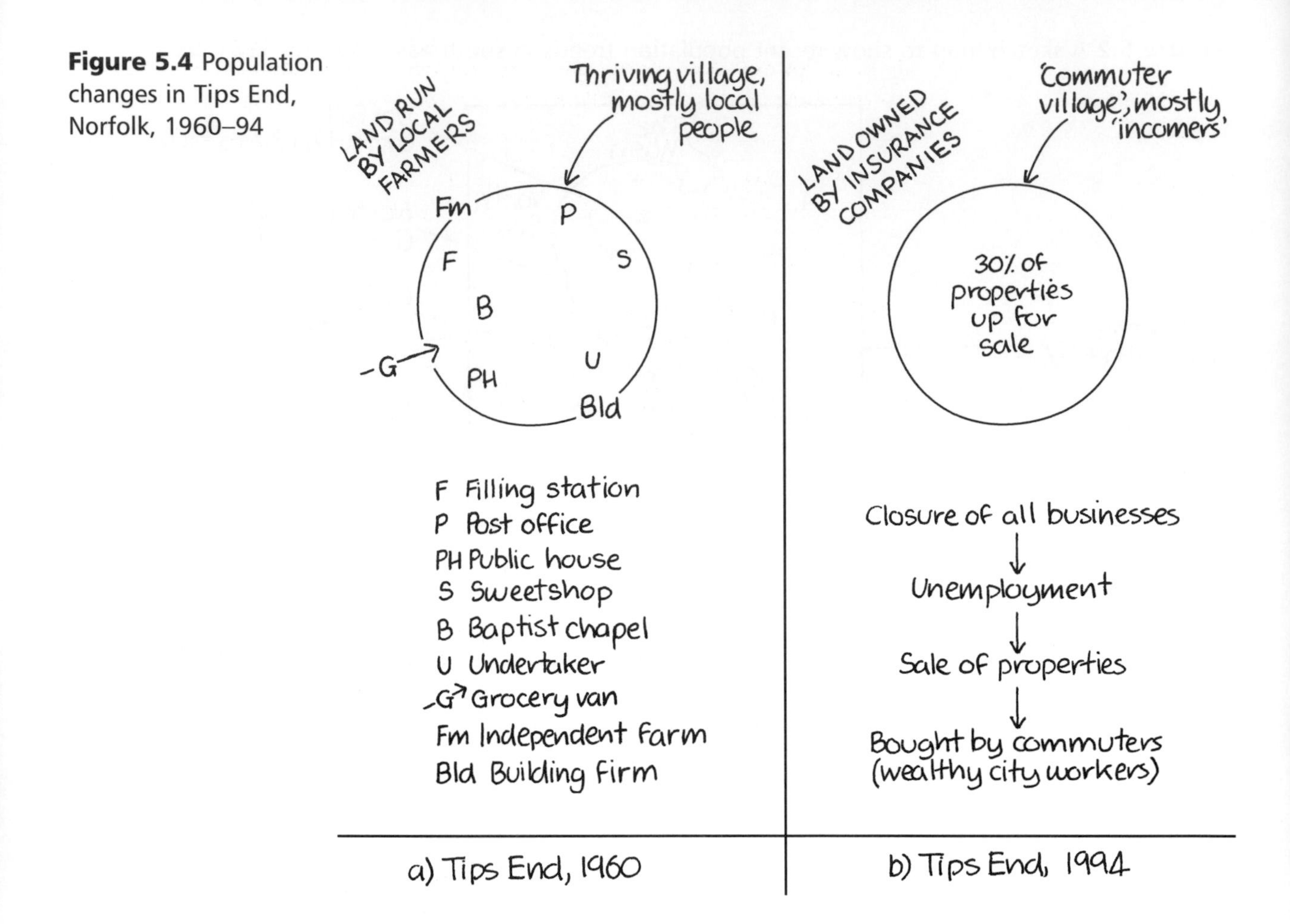

Figure 5.4 Population changes in Tips End, Norfolk, 1960–94

SECTION E

Using a case study

Having simplified and learned the facts of the case study, you are now in a position to use it in a variety of ways. Let us look at two different essay titles where you might employ this case study (notes on planning essays are found in **Chapter 4**).

a) *'In developed countries, migration is now mainly from urban to rural areas.' Discuss, with reference to actual examples.*

b) *Using examples, examine the claim that changing employment structures often lead to major spatial re-organisation.*

The two essays are from different parts of the syllabus but because you have simplified your case study, it would be easy to use it in either context. This is how it might be planned into the two answers.

Plan a: 'In developed countries, migration is now mainly from urban to rural areas.' Discuss, with reference to actual examples.

Introduction
Define migration in the context of 'urban' and 'rural'.

Expansion

Step 1 UK 1981–91 growth in rural areas surrounding London. Decline in London's population. Mainly due to movement from London to countryside, but also movement from some rural areas, e.g. Tips End, and to urban areas surrounding London, e.g. Cambridge.

Annotated map.

Step 2 France 1981–now. Depopulation in Central Paris – relocation of businesses, growth of commuting (high-speed transport to outlying areas). Growth in countryside e.g. Orléans (100km from Paris). But also rural depopulation (farm re-organisation, development of regional hubs for new industries, lack of facilities for the young, etc.) and growth of urban areas, e.g. Lille (Eurotunnel terminus, science city, redevelopment of old industrial sites).

Annotated map.

Conclusion
Basically true. The overall movement is to move house from urban to rural, but people commute from rural to urban for work and services. There are many instances of villages declining and towns growing within this pattern.

Note: this is a basic outline. A good answer might well contain an American or an Asian example as well.

Plan b: Using examples, examine the claim that changing employment structures often lead to major spatial re-organisation.

Introduction
Define 'employment structure' in terms of primary, secondary, tertiary and quaternary as well as modern and traditional industries. Spatial re-organisation refers to where it is located now as opposed to where it was before.

Expansion
Step 1 UK – decline of traditional rural industries as mechanisation and rationalisation affect farms. Greater mobility allows country-dwellers to choose where they shop and they often

choose stores in nearby large towns – rural services decline. Result – decline in rural population. Greater mobility also allows urban population to live in the country and commute to the town to work. Commuters also find better quality of life in the countryside. Result – growth of rural population at the expense of the urban population (UK 1981–91).

Sketch map to show distribution changes.

Step 2 Migrant workers in France. End of French colonial rule especially in North Africa meant workers from the developing countries (e.g. Algeria, Morocco, Tunisia) migrated to France, especially around Marseilles, to find work. Migrants, mainly young males, later joined by the rest of the family. Result – the expansion of high-density suburban developments around Marseilles and later northern cities such as Paris.

Other potential examples – government-inspired industrial change in such places as the new towns led to the movement of population from central city areas to places such as Corby to work in the iron and steel industry. Decline of specialist industries, e.g. shipbuilding in the North East of England – depopulation as skilled industrial workers moved to find new industrial employment elsewhere, e.g. the car industry.

Conclusion
There have been major changes in population density and distribution as a result of changing employment, especially when uneven development occurs in a country. It can be reversed (by government regional development policies) but not completely so.

These two plans show how a thorough, detailed case study can be applied equally well in different answers. It is essential to have a spread of detailed case studies, but depth is also vital to allow you to use them flexibly.

In answers such as these, it is advisable to refer to at least two reasonably detailed case studies to illustrate the general points you are making. Don't forget, however, that other case studies in very different parts of the subject can be used to show your breadth of information. For example, in the second question, you could refer to examples of many other factors, apart from employment (i.e. economic activity) that lead to spatial re-organisation. These could be physical factors (e.g. vulcanicity – the migration from Montserrat), changes in infrastructure (e.g. the possibility of living in one location and working in another due to advances in transport and communications) or political factors (e.g. ethnic cleansing in Bosnia). You would not need to say much about them, but this sort of cross-referencing should always be encouraged. In this case, you might use the three references just quoted to put the importance of changing employment structures in context. Remember that, important though it is, it is not the only factor affecting spatial reorganisation.

Review

2 Now try these exercises using the model suggested above for preparing your case studies.
  a Prepare revision notes and annotated maps for one of your most detailed case studies.
  b Make a list of the themes for which the case study may be relevant as illustrative material.
  c Write detailed notes for an answer to a question (either your own or taken from a past exam paper) relating to one of the themes you have identified in **(b)** and using your case study.

SECTION F

Summing up

A good case study:

- gives precise detail and is not vague
- benefits from supporting maps and/or diagrams, particularly if they clarify and simplify
- is up to date
- utilises your own experience, particularly the content of your personal investigative project
- is prepared so that it can be used in a variety of essay answers.

In collecting your case studies, it is vital that you are always clear about:

- what syllabus theme(s) each relates to
- what specific point(s) within the theme each supports.

Constantly review your collection and don't be frightened to weed out case studies as they are superseded by better ones. An overload of case studies can be as damaging as having too few.

CHAPTER

6 Using maps and diagrams

In this chapter you will learn to:

- see maps and diagrams as an integral part of an examination answer or essay
- spot whether a particular diagram is relevant or not
- check against a key list to see that all the requirements of a good illustration have been met
- impress examiners out of all proportion to the value of the diagram.

A Chief Examiner recently commented:

> *We are always pleased to read scripts where candidates are prepared to display their competence in drawing diagrams, graphs and maps. These key geographical skills are nowhere near as well developed as they once were.*

In other words, if students can learn to include well-drawn and relevant illustrations in their answers, they stand a chance of creating a very favourable impression.

SECTION A

Make sure the diagram is relevant

All too often, a student explains a particular point and then draws a diagram covering exactly the same material – or the other way round. The examiner can only reward the making of a relevant, correct point once. So half the student's effort has been wasted.

To avoid this trap, plan ahead. From your essay plan (**Chapter 4**) you know the points you are trying to make. You then decide which of those points you intend to illustrate. Once this is done, then let your writing set the scene. The last sentence you write before the diagram should be interchangeable with the title of the diagram. After the illustration, you should not say 'as the diagram shows', but comment on it in some way that gives additional value. You might quote actual examples, for instance, or describe any interrelationships revealed by your drawing. This is best shown by an example. Let's assume that part of your essay on tourism requires you to examine its economic impacts.

> *The scale of the economic impact of tourism on an area depends on a number of factors.*

As well as economic benefits, there can be economic disadvantages. Frequently, tourism can lead to increased inflation, increased pressure to import, and rising land values that affect the cost of local housing.

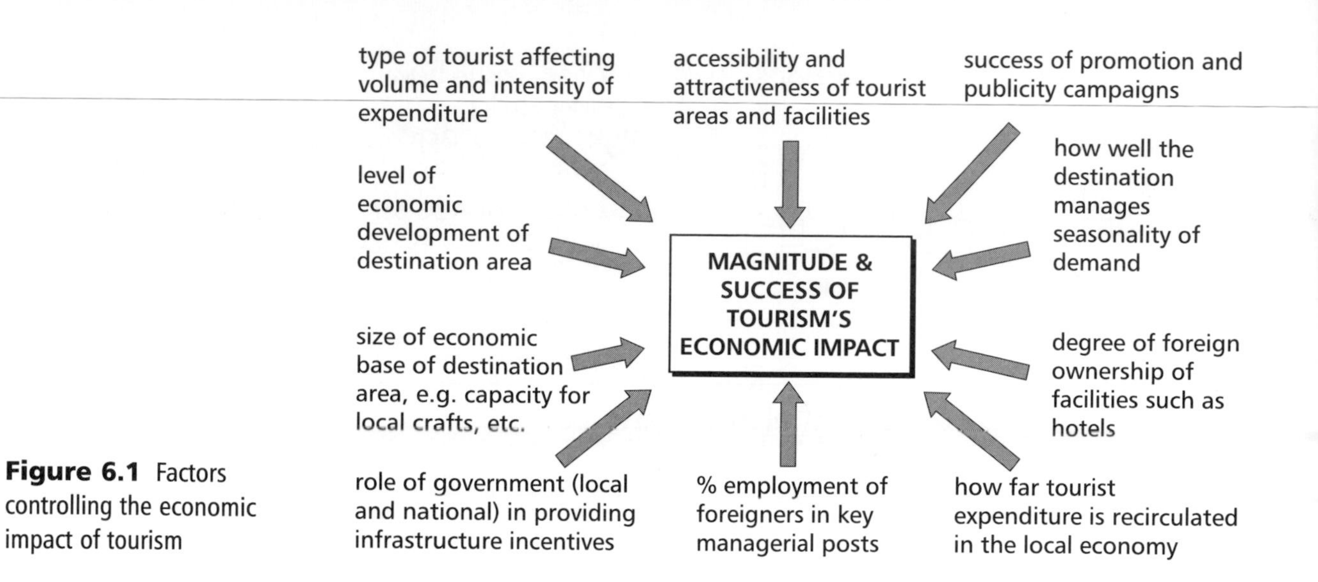

Figure 6.1 Factors controlling the economic impact of tourism

This example sets up the title in one short sentence. Diagram **6.1** gives ten factors affecting the magnitude and success of tourism's economic impact. Then, rather than comment on the labels (which are, after all, self-explanatory), it introduces the new point that the same factor can have both negative and positive results. If you read the full passage (*Environment and People* page 407), you will see that it then gives examples to show how the factors work together in some examples (such as the Alps, Lake Balaton in Hungary and the area surrounding the Pyramids in Egypt). The points made on the diagram are only made once.

SECTION B

Make sure the diagram is important

Diagrams work best when they illustrate complex interrelationships, time series and spatial layouts. They can be wasted if:

- they illustrate something too insignificant
- they make a point that can be written in one or two sentences
- they are not labelled properly.

Figure 6.2 The causes of local winds

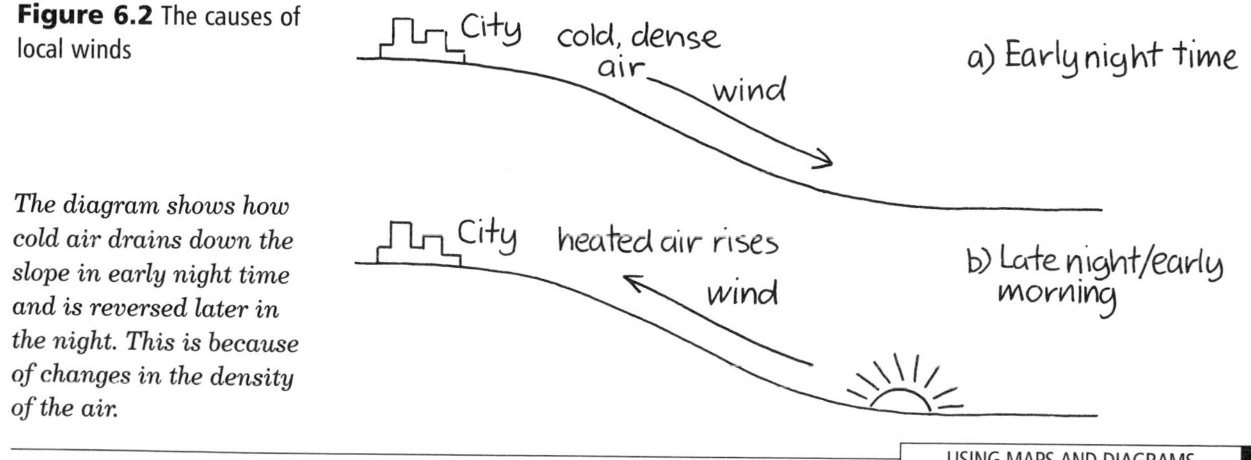

The diagram shows how cold air drains down the slope in early night time and is reversed later in the night. This is because of changes in the density of the air.

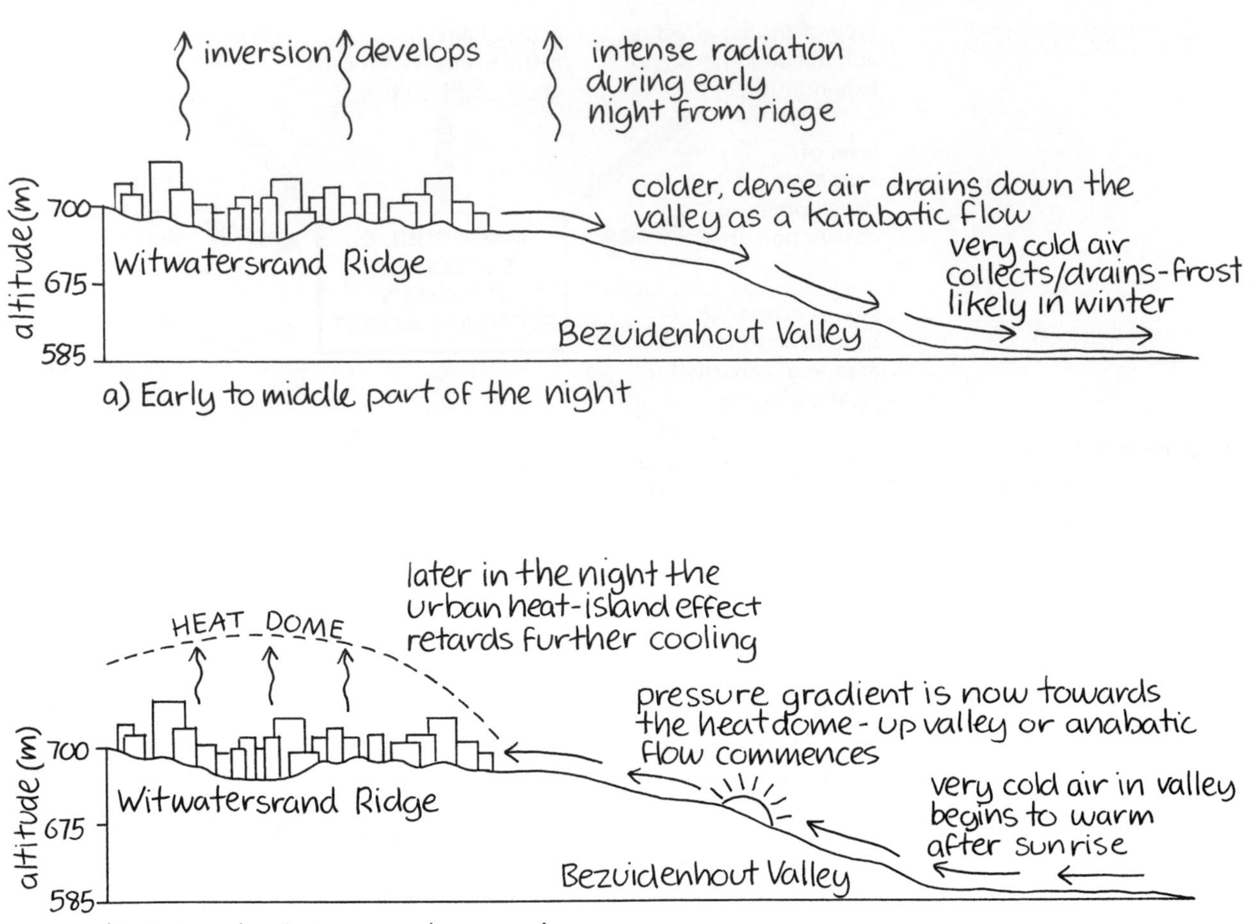

Figure 6.3 The formation of 'country breezes' in the Johannesburg area

The reversal of winds over a 24-hour period can cause major modifications to the local climate, as in the case of Johannesburg, South Africa.

In an area where temperatures can reach 30°C on a hot summer's day, the cooling effect of katabatic winds is most welcome.

Again, let us look at an example. First, **6.2** on page 57 is a poor use of a diagram in an essay answer to a question on local winds. This example is about as vague as they come! The few, general labels on the diagram are repeated in the vague text. The whole diagram is wasted.

The same example could be approached in a much more constructive way.

In the second case, the actual example has been used as an integral part of the diagram (**6.3**). The title adds the information that this particular reversal of winds is known as 'country breezes' and the subsequent sentence adds the detail that they have a cooling effect in an area that can get particularly hot. There is no repetition and the labels on the second pair of diagrams are much more detailed than they were on the first pair.

SECTION C

Make sure the diagram is complete

Here is the checklist you were promised. A good illustration should include:

- a title
- clear, detailed labels
- a key
- a scale (or approximate scale)
- a north point (if relevant).

Although this is more a matter of choice, it helps you to present clear and tidy maps and diagrams if you give them all a ruled border. This does not take long and significantly improves appearance. It avoids you running your text right up to the diagram. If you do that it will reduce the significance of the illustration and make it look untidy. Upgrading your diagrams (and maps) can be achieved by:

- using colour
- printing instead of writing
- labelling with points that refer to the text.

On this last point, if you label a point 'X' on the diagram, you can ensure that the diagram is fully integrated into the written answer by writing a sentence in the text referring to X. For example, you could say:

> *As shown at point X in the diagram, London grew up at a point where the River Thames could be easily crossed.*

This is a very good technique, apart from the title trick we have already mentioned, to ensure that the text and diagram work together and do not repeat information.

SECTION D

Examples of diagram styles

Let us now look in more detail at some other types of diagrams.

PRIMARY PRODUCER		PRIMARY CONSUMER		SECONDARY CONSUMER
Plant matter – tropical grasses	→	Zebra	→	Lion

Figure 6.4 A simplified food chain

Simple connections

Rather than write about the relationships between producers and consumers in a savanna ecosystem, you might punctuate your text by suggesting the connections in a simple diagram (**6.4**). You would have to write considerable explanation to go with this diagram.

If, however, you were to add more useful dimensions to this diagram, by suggesting not just a linkage between them but a hierarchy, and setting it in a regional context, you would probably make better use of the opportunity (**6.5**).

Figure 6.5 The relationship between producers and consumers in a savanna ecosystem

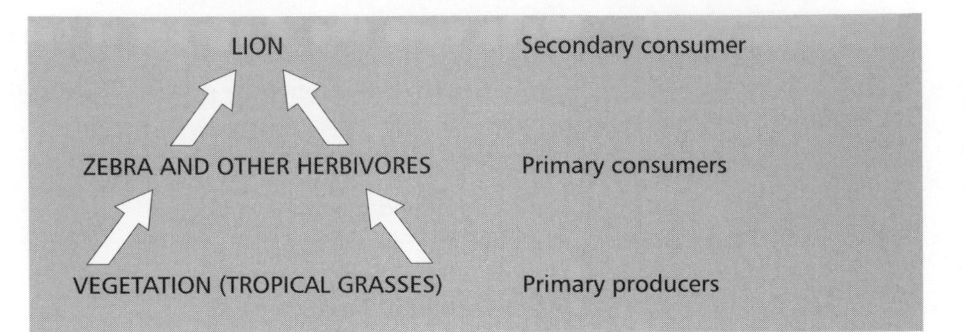

Fluid connections

Sometimes, feedback from a series of actions or natural events can have an effect on other actions or events which continue to develop in a particular direction as a result. It is helpful in such instances to see the result in terms of the way we might describe it: 'an upward or downward spiral', 'a vicious cycle', 'a knock-on effect', 'feedback', and so on. Figure **6.6** shows how we might illustrate the negative impacts of migration on peripheral regions as a 'downward spiral'.

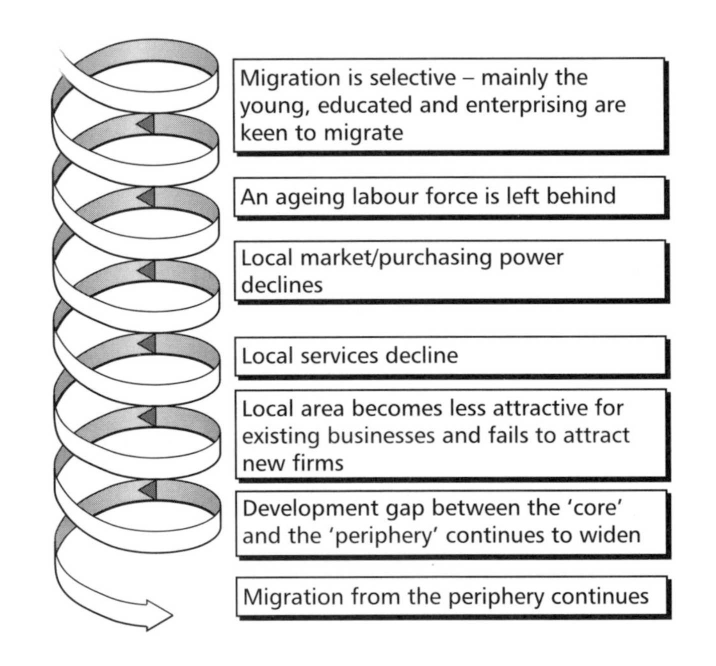

Figure 6.6 A downward spiral – backwash and the impact of migration on peripheral areas

Pictorial representations

If you have an artistic ability (and many students do have) you might like to lighten the examiner's day by adding some simple drawings to your diagrams. Please do not make them a time-consuming work of art, but they can add a level of interest and understanding that words and arrows fail to do. An example, again of the food chain (now expressed as the more complex 'food web') is shown in **6.7**.

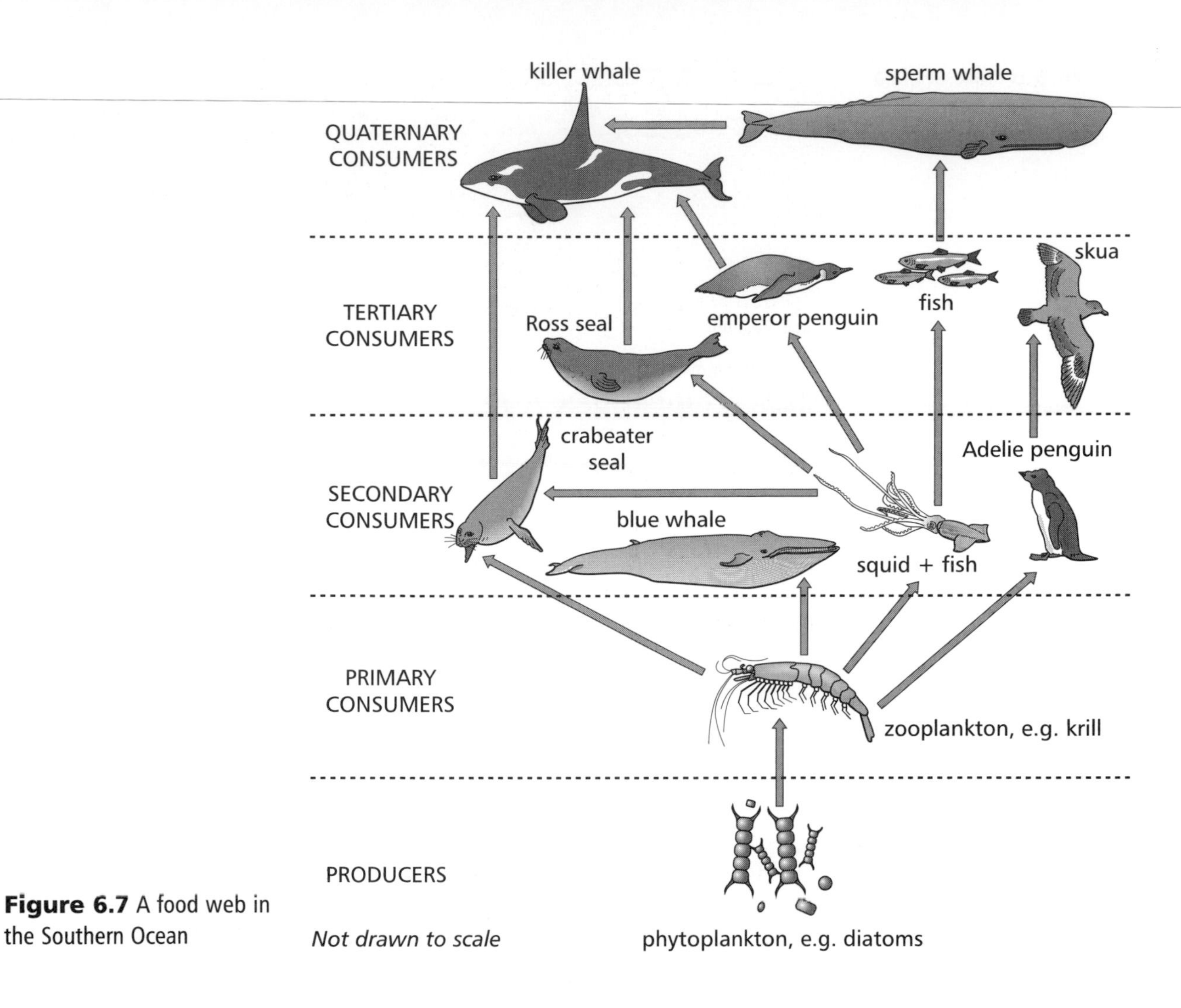

Figure 6.7 A food web in the Southern Ocean

You will be able to see the value of such a diagram if, using the diagram alone, you try to answer the question:

What would be the effects of harvesting large quantities of krill from the Southern Ocean?

You will be able to give a lot of detail in your answer simply by using **6.7** as your source. This is how a good diagram works. At its best, a diagram is a sort of shorthand. It can show, with a few well-chosen labels and drawings, relationships that would otherwise take many sentences to explain.

Illustrating dynamic processes

Movement is very difficult to explain in words, particularly when several opposing movements may contribute to one process. Diagram **6.8** overleaf shows the processes operating in a well-developed thunderstorm cloud. Try to put those processes into words. This is a very good example of a 'picture being worth a thousand words'. Without a diagram, it is very difficult to describe all of the processes shown and the relationships between them.

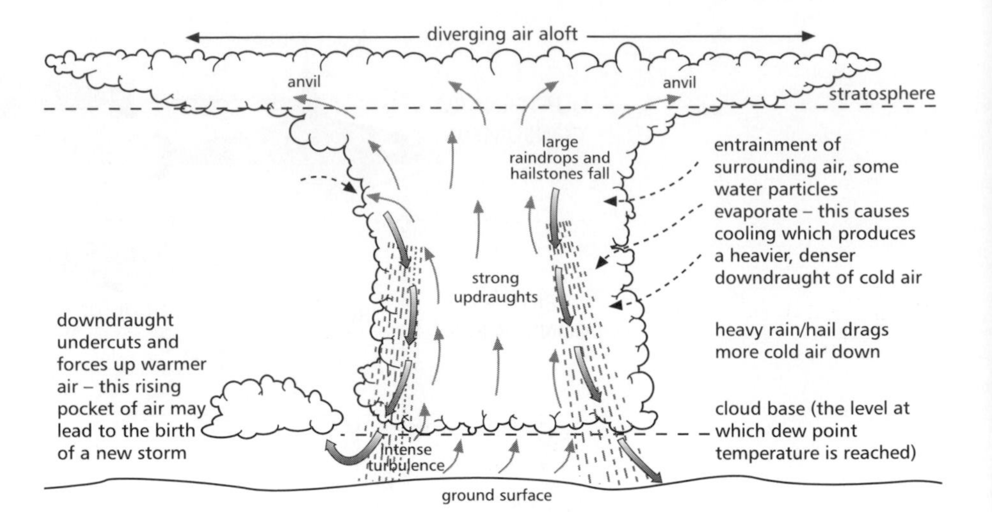

Figure 6.8 Processes in a well-developed thunderstorm cloud

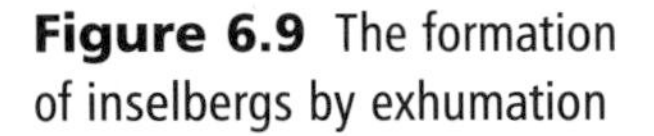

Figure 6.9 The formation of inselbergs by exhumation

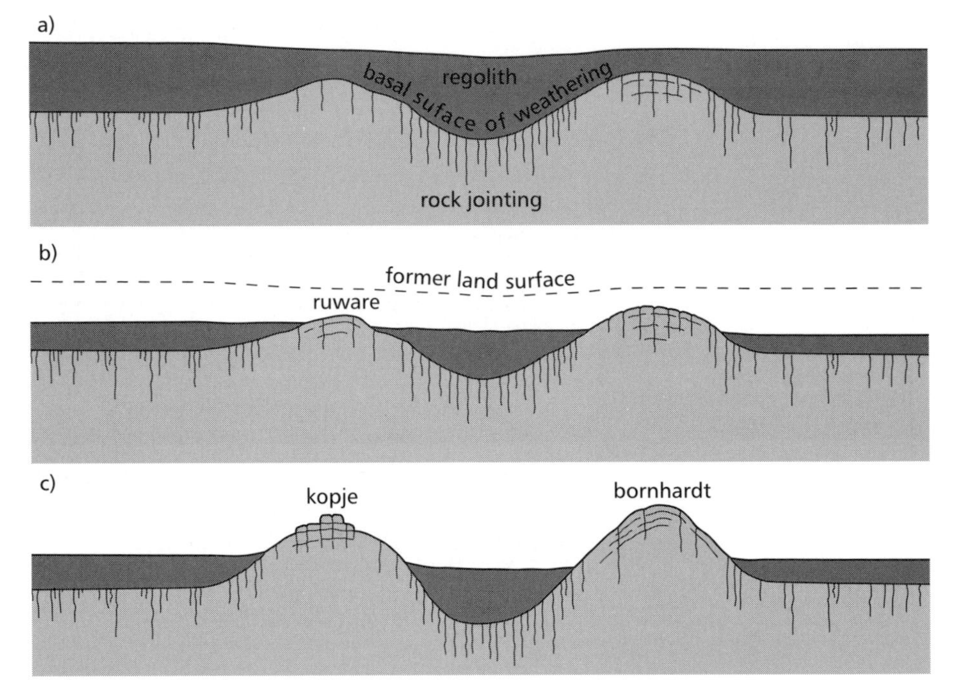

Similarly, a series of diagrams can be used to show development over time. The diagrams in **6.9**, also from *Environment and People*, show the developments of hills in semi-arid areas.

SECTION E

Using sketch maps

The same rules as we have just discussed for diagrams apply to sketch maps. In an essay answer, they should appear at a relevant point and should not duplicate what you have already said but should add something to the answer. They should be clearly drawn, separated from the text by a ruled boundary and given a title that follows on from the text itself.

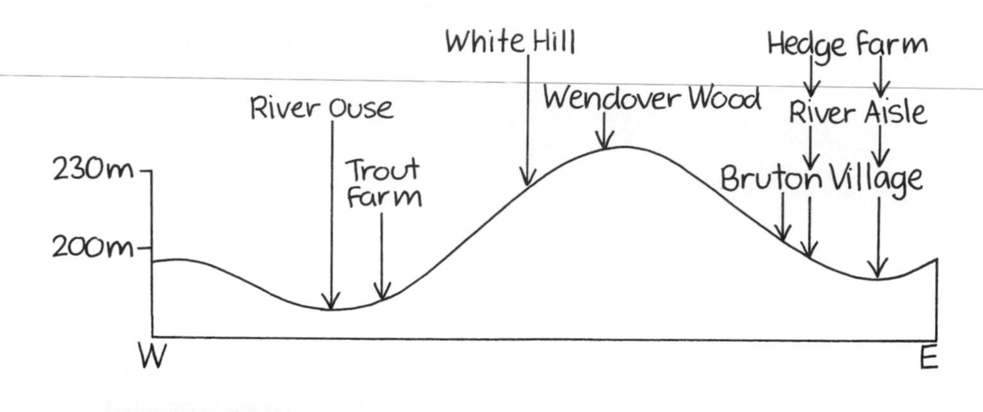

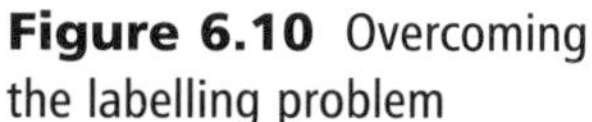

Figure 6.10 Overcoming the labelling problem

Review

1 Redraw **6.9** to show how the landscape has evolved, adding the labels below in the correct places. Labels on a diagram should always be written horizontally (so that it can be read easily). If necessary the diagram should be extended to accommodate the labels, with an arrow directed at the point to which the label refers. An example has been completed for you in **6.10**.

The labels for your diagram are:

a closely spaced joints
ground surface
deep weathering by chemical means

b removal of regolith by water and wind
exposure of basal surface of weathering

c continued weathering of finely jointed rock beneath regolith
flat surface (pediplain)
kopjes and bornhardts are two types of inselberg

As you complete this exercise, you will find that labels compete for space. Solve this by placing some at a higher level than others, but remember to keep the printing horizontal.

An example of a sketch map is given in **6.11** on page 64. It also shows how a complex map of land use in central Tokyo (**6.11a**) can be simplified to turn it into a model, something that you may be able to remember for an examination (**6.11b**). The detailed map would obviously be beyond accurate memory and there would not be enough time to reproduce it in this detail anyway. Sketch map **6.11b** might be used to answer the question:

'To what extent does the pattern of land use in an Asian city differ from that you might expect find in a major European city?'

Example answer

A model of central Tokyo reveals that the focus of the land-use pattern is the port on Tokyo Bay. Zones of different use tend to run north–south across the area and the western side of the city is almost a mirror-image of the east. A Western city would typically be zoned around the CBD.'

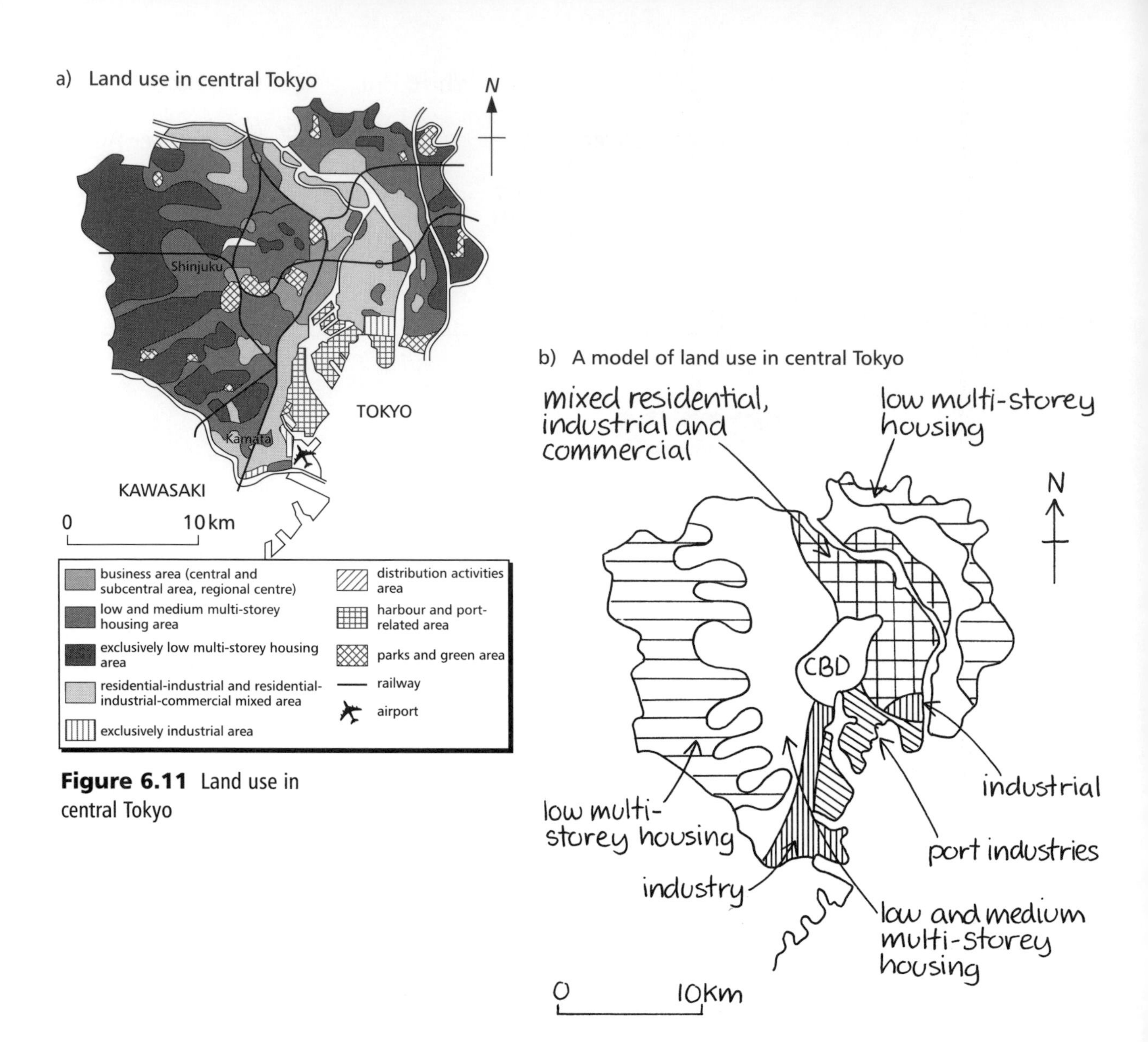

Figure 6.11 Land use in central Tokyo

Annotated sketch maps

One of the most useful types of sketch map is one that is fully annotated. It can provide an aid to remembering a case study, is useful for summarising your notes and ensures that you keep things in a geographical (i.e. spatial) context. Sometimes, examination questions can be answered almost solely with an annotated map.

Your sketch map should occupy the centre of a page and should be drawn boldly to show the relationships between features. The labels for these features should be neatly written and then a box placed around them to separate them from the other labels. In a complex map, you might have quite a few labels. An example is given in **6.12**.

Review

2 a To practise this technique for yourself, draw a copy of the population density map of Egypt on page 66 (**6.13**). Then use the paragraph describing and explaining the population distribution to compile your revision notes version. Use **6.12** as a model.

b Find a good case study in your notes. Draw a base sketch map and then label it to transfer the case-study information to the map.

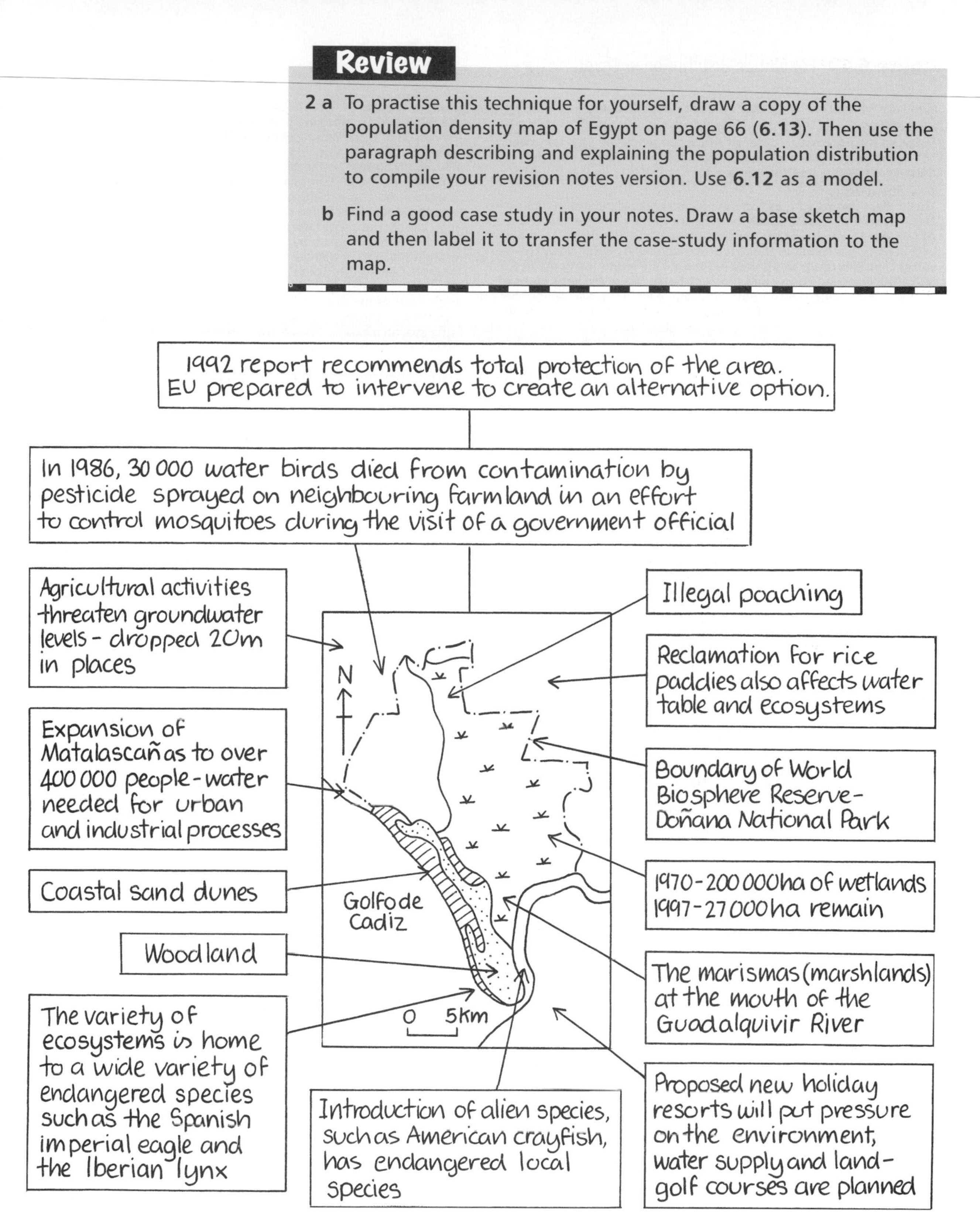

Figure 6.12 An annotated sketch map of the Coto Doñana wetlands, Spain (*Environment and People*, page 235)

Figure 6.13 Population distribution in Egypt

'Describe and explain the density and distribution of population in Egypt.'

Introduction

Egypt, in the north-east corner of Africa bordering the Mediterranean Sea, has some of the most densely populated and some of the least densely populated areas in the world.

Describe density

The highest density of population (over 500 people per km^2) is found in the area around Cairo and northwards along the two main distributaries of the river Nile towards the Mediterranean Sea. High densities of over 100 per km^2 are found in the rest of the delta and inland along the Nile valley. Densities of up to 50 people per km^2 are found along the Red Sea and Mediterranean coasts and the Suez Canal. There are large areas of very low population density both west and east of the Nile valley. There is a sudden division between the high densities of the Nile valley and the low densities which are found on either side of it.

Describe distribution

In terms of distribution, the high-density population areas form linear zones through the country, along the Nile itself, along the banks of the Suez Canal and along the coasts of the Red Sea and the Mediterranean Sea. The lowest-density areas form continuous zones across the rest of the country.

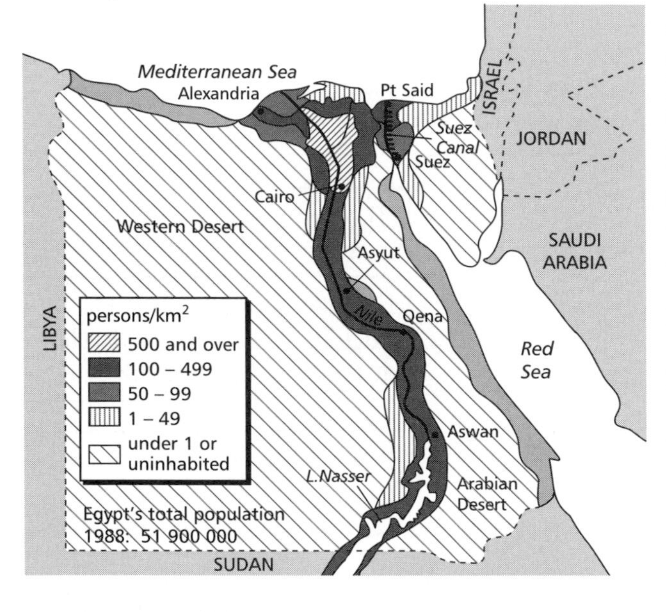

Explain density

The high-density areas are principally explained by the presence of fertile soil or by communications and trade routes. Along the Nile valley, farmland is particularly productive. The relief is flat, the soil is alluvial (deposited by the Nile in flood and full of minerals) and therefore rich, and there is a constant water supply (even if irrigation is a laborious chore in the growing season). The climate is hot all year and allows for up to three crops annually. Consequently there is a high concentration of farmers in these areas. Along the Nile itself, which is a major waterway, trading settlements have been established. This is also the case on the Mediterranean coast, the Red Sea coast and in the Suez Canal area. These developments lead to moderate population densities. The low-density areas represent the high lands of the Arabian Desert, and the Western and Arabian Deserts themselves. In these areas there are extreme temperatures, little available water, difficult rocky and sandy terrain and few natural resources. Where these do occur, as in the oilfields along the Red Sea coast and west of Alexandria and in the oases (e.g. Kharga and Dakhla Oasis west of Luxor), population densities are slightly higher. The greatest population densities of all are now found in the major towns where industry (Cairo), trade (Suez) or tourism (Giza) have led to concentration.

Explain distribution

The linear distributions of high-density population are linked to the communications and agricultural activities along the river Nile, the trading artery of the Suez Canal and the developments along both the Mediterranean and Red Sea coasts. The large areas of relatively low population correlate with the inhospitable desert areas and the abrupt break between high and low-density distributions reflects the limits imposed by nature on further human development given the present level of technology, especially in water exploitation. Attempts have been made to expand the area under cultivation, for example by using water from Lake Nasser (impounded behind the Aswan High Dam), but these have only emphasised the sharp break between densely populated farming regions and almost unpopulated desert.

The large areas of low density are explained by the climatic conditions prevailing there. The deserts coincide almost exactly with the areas of lowest density, but this is relieved in a few places where other attributes, such as trade routes, the availability of water or oil deposits, make it worth while for people to live in the area, even though they have to pay heavily for imported water and foodstuffs (except in the case of oases).

Conclusion

Egypt has a very well-defined distribution of areas of different population densities. It also has large areas which, given the technology, could be populated in the future. However, with the predicted accentuation of dry areas (due to warming under the greenhouse effect), the distribution is likely to continue to reflect great differences.

SECTION F

Using graphs

A graph can also be drawn quite easily in an examination situation and will very effectively illustrate, for example, the relationship between two variables. The graph **6.14** clearly shows this for two of the indicators frequently used for measuring economic development. Note that there is no need to quantify or add numerical values to the axes and it may not even be necessary to name the countries shown by the dots. It is the **relationship** that you are trying to illustrate.

Changes or sequences over time can also be shown in diagrammatic or graphic form. Every A-level student should be able to reproduce the **demographic transition model** with a considerable degree of accuracy. Similarly, a simply drawn population pyramid can prove to the examiner that you understand the effect that changes in fertility, mortality and the migration balance have on population structure (**6.15**). Note that there has been no attempt to add any detailed numerical values to this pyramid for a coastal resort in the UK; in this case you are trying to illustrate the impact of time on the present population structure.

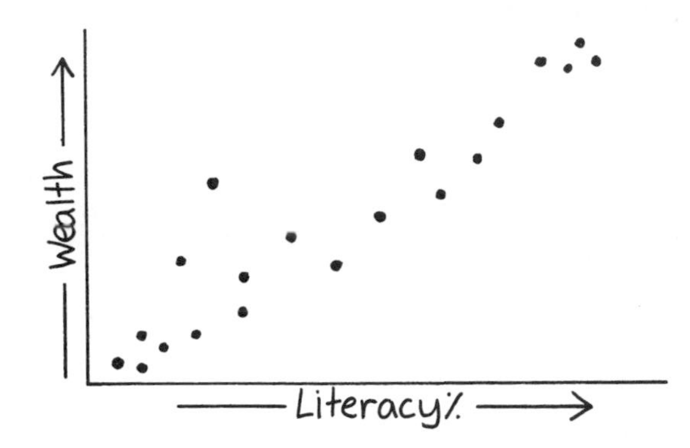

Figure 6.14 Scattergraph showing the relationship between wealth and literacy

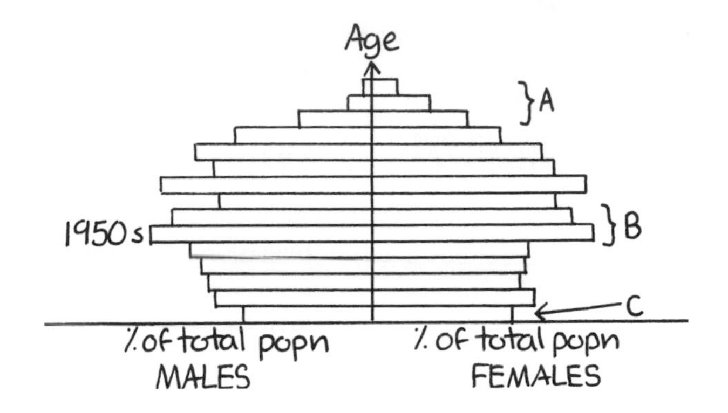

Figure 6.15 Population pyramid for a UK coastal resort, 1990

Review

3 How would you explain the changes in population structure that have occurred at points A, B and C on graph **6.15**? Note that you could put A, B and C as labels on the graph to ensure that it is integrated into the text when you explain them. See also **Chapter 7** for help on interpreting graphs.

SECTION G

Summing up

Please remember the following tips:

- Make your maps and diagrams relevant and meaningful.
- Take plenty of space for the drawing.
- Label it carefully.
- Remember – title, key, north point, scale, border and shading.
- Make sure your diagram is an integral part of your writing.

In addition, it is necessary to sound two cautionary notes:

- Do not get too involved in trying to produce maps and diagrams of artistic excellence or intricate detail. This can be both counter-productive and self-penalising. Examiners are not artists. All they will assess is the degree to which you use these skills to convey the geographical knowledge and understanding you have that is relevant to a particular question.
- Do not spend an undue amount of time on this aspect of your answer.

CHAPTER 7

Improving your data-response skills

SECTION A

What is data response?

The term **data response** is applied in A-level Geography to those questions based on or built round some form of visual material (sometimes referred to as **stimulus response**). That material may range from newspaper articles and cartoons, through statistical tables, graphs, maps and diagrams to photographs and satellite images. You might be asked to interpret a map, establish the relationships shown by a graph or identify key concepts or ideas conveyed by a diagram. Less frequently, you might be asked to provide a rather open-ended analysis of a range of stimulus materials. All the questions are designed to assess two things:

- your knowledge of particular subject areas, especially your grasp of terminology, basic concepts and ideas
- your ability to read and interpret data presented in a variety of forms.

The latter is usually assessed by the examination boards in one or both of two ways:

- by structured, short-answer questions
- by a decision-making exercise.

This chapter tries to improve the skills you need to cope with the first type of assessment. **Chapter 8** deals with the second. In addition, it is worth pointing out that the personal enquiry (**Chapter 9**) also requires you to demonstrate that you can present data in an appropriate form, as well as properly interpret it.

SECTION B

Structured short-answer questions

Most A-level Geography examinations these days set structured short-answer questions that involve varying degrees of data response. Such questions are usually subdivided into parts, each requiring a brief response and each often building on its predecessor. Often there is an incline of difficulty as you work your way through the sequence of parts. With some boards, there is a question book with limited space set aside for each part of your answers. Woe betide you if you overrun the allocated space! In some instances, the visual material is used as an initial stimulus. In others, the map or diagram comes later and is there to test not only your ability to understand and interpret it, but also your grasp of basic concepts.

A student who is good at writing essays is not necessarily as good at tackling structured, data-response questions. Answering them has its own set of skills and techniques, but they are fairly straightforward to master. Here are some tips.

Read the question thoroughly

Under the stress of examinations, it is easy to read questions hurriedly and carelessly. Try to hold back and for each question double-check that you are clear as to the precise topic being examined. Do you feel that you have the requisite knowledge and understanding? Are you familiar with the nature of the stimulus material being used?

Watch the command words

Having decided that you can tackle a particular question, the next step is to make sure that you understand exactly what you are being asked to do. The question will have a series of command words in it, such as 'state', 'describe', 'list', 'explain', 'justify', and so on (see **Chapter 10, Section C**). Each of these command words makes a specific request.

For example, the question 'List the factors that make the city of Oxford prone to flooding' requires nothing more than a series of brief statements:

- *Oxford is low-lying.*
- *It is built around the confluence of two rivers.*
- *The local rocks are impermeable.*
- *Human activity has increased the flood risk.*

By contrast, the question 'Describe Oxford's flood problem' looks for more detail and full sentences. The answer might read:

> *Oxford is affected by the flooding of the rivers Thames and Cherwell which meet in the centre of Oxford. The Thames floods most winters, while the Cherwell floods more often. Summer flash floods are also a problem. The areas of the city most at risk are along the banks of both rivers. These areas are now avoided by housing and used mainly for recreation or farming.*

If the question were 'Explain Oxford's flood problem', then again an answer in continuous prose is required. It might proceed as follows:

> *Oxford suffers from many floods because two rivers meet there. This means that a lot of water passes through a small area. In addition, much of the area is underlain by clay. Clay is an impermeable rock, which means that water flows over the surface rather than sinks in. Because of the built-up area, runoff into the rivers is speeded up by sewers and drains. The short time-lag also increases the risk of flooding.*

Make enough points

If we were tackling the first version of the question on Oxford flooding, we might worry about the number of factors that we should list. The examiners might have been more helpful and stipulated the number. Since they have not, then we can only be guided by two things:

- the amount of space allocated in the answer book
- the number of marks allocated to that part of the question.

In the case of those examination boards that do not provide a special answer book, then you will have to use the second indicator. If 4 marks were available, then it would be reasonable to think that the concise statement of four factors was all that was required.

Make use of the stimulus material

The maps, graphs, photographs or newspaper cuttings that are an integral part of most structured, short-answer questions are there to put you on the right track. In addition, they are often there to be analysed. It is all too easy to forget the stimulus materials and to refer to other examples you have studied. Don't be frightened that you are seeing information for the first time. The whole of your A-level training is to prepare you to be able to analyse new geographical information. Trust your training and refer to the stimulus material to support your answers as appropriate.

Be concise, neat and tidy

There is a common misconception that a 'short' answer is a 'hurried' or a 'that'll do' answer. Quite the reverse is the case. If you are trying to get a point across succinctly, you must be very clear. Think carefully before you write. You cannot afford to do a lot of crossing out and re-writing, partly because of the time factor and partly because of the fact that you may well be writing in an answer book with a specific allocation of space for each part of the structured question. If the latter applies, then be sure to keep to the lined spaces provided. *Do not* overspill and try to be clever by inserting two lines of your own writing for each line in the answer book! Do not waste words – it is surprising how many examination candidates waste time and effort repeating the question.

For further advice on this and other types of examination paper have a look at **Chapter 10**. Let us now look at the skills and materials involved in data-response.

SECTION C

Analysing maps

The maps in **7.1** show the distribution of employment in the food industry in the Netherlands. The number employed gives a good guide to the relative importance of the industry within the divisions of each province. But it hides the fact that some food industries are more labour intensive than others. So be careful with your analysis.

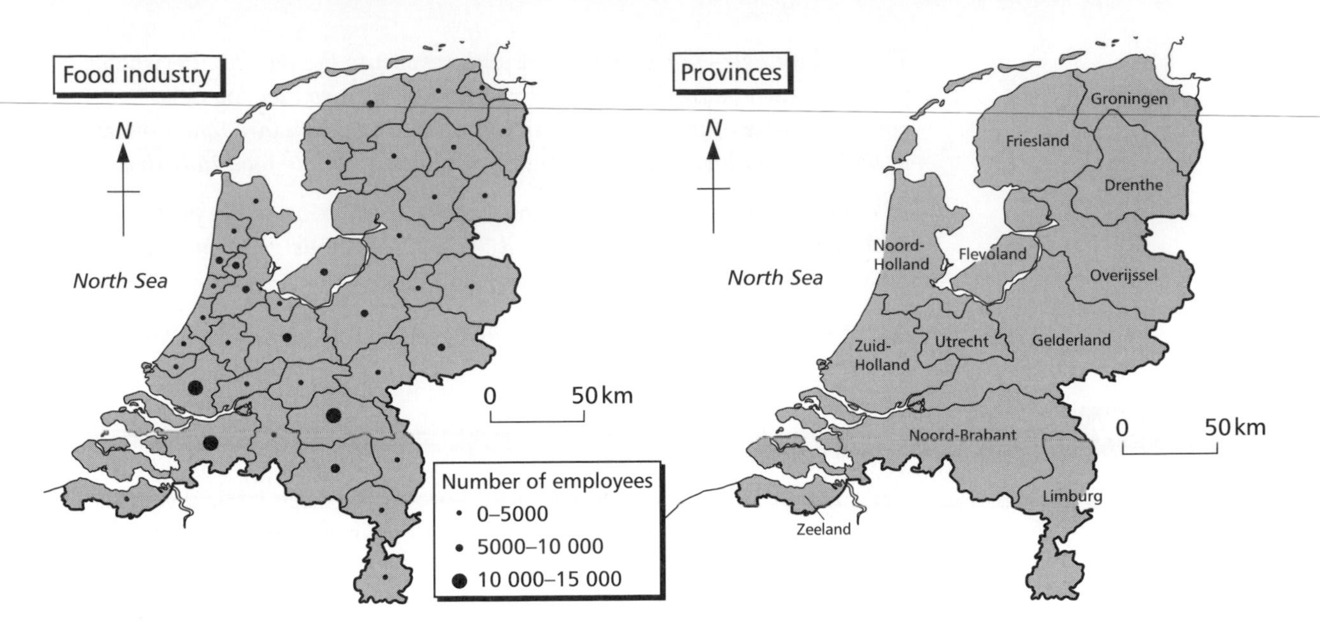

Figure 7.1 The distribution of employment in the food industry in the Netherlands

Let's suppose that the question is as follows:

a Describe the distribution of employment in the food industry in the Netherlands.

b Identify the factors that have influenced the distribution pattern.

a Description

This requires you to establish when the distribution is even or uneven. Look for concentrations and absences, and location with respect to particular geographic features (rivers, borders, etc.). So, in this case:

- even distribution – food industry found in all states, no absences at a provincial level
- up to 10 000 employed in most states, but larger concentrations in the south (the provinces of Zuid-Holland and Noord-Brabant)
- Rhine estuary and valley hold concentrations, near border with Belgium.

Note that although we have located the concentrations with respect to the Rhine, this is recorded as a descriptive feature rather than an explanation (the latter is not required here). If we were to say that the concentration was there because of the river, this would be an explanation. Be alive to this subtle, but important, difference.

b Explanatory factors

Look back to the 'skeleton' in **Chapter 3, Section H**. This gives you a useful checklist of things that might help to explain the distribution you have described. Look for links with any of the factors, for example:

The food industry is partly located with respect to the market. Perishable products, such as fresh bread and vegetables, are produced near to concentrations of people. Population densities are high throughout most of the Netherlands, hence the 'underlying spread' of the food industry.

In addition, there are concentrations, particularly around the port of Rotterdam (break-of-bulk point) and in areas of intensive farming such as Noord-Brabant (processing of farm products).

Lower employment figures occur in more rural areas and where the farming is less intensive.

Review

1 Study map **7.2** showing the global distribution of manufacturing.

a Identify the salient features of the distribution. **b** Suggest an explanation for the features you have identified in (**a**).

Here is some help.

a Describe the pattern, relating high values to continents, coastal or interior locations, hemispheres or latitudes.

b Note that there are areas of high value added (clues: economically more developed countries or EMDCs, large countries) as the figures are not per capita; areas of intermediate value added (clues: tiger economies, newly-industrialised countries or NICs) and areas with low value added (clue: economically less developed countries or ELDCs).

Write a paragraph for each part, giving a comprehensive coverage with located examples and precise numerical statements. Make sure you use the key intelligently, not simply by repeating a list of countries or areas and their value added, but by giving examples to illustrate the generalisations you have made (e.g. the NICs, such as Singapore, added more value in terms of manufacturing – about US$10 million in 1988 – than countries such as New Zealand or Uruguay).

Before you start, plan your answer for a couple of minutes. In particular, don't forget Europe in its isolated box. Show that you understand what 'value added' means. Make the point that sophisticated industries such as aircraft manufacture add more value than industries such as brewing. Exporting raw materials adds no value at all.

SECTION D

Interpreting graphs

There are many types of graph that you may encounter in data response, but we look at the three most common types to help you with your planning. You can adapt the ideas to other types of graph by practising on the ones found in any good textbook.

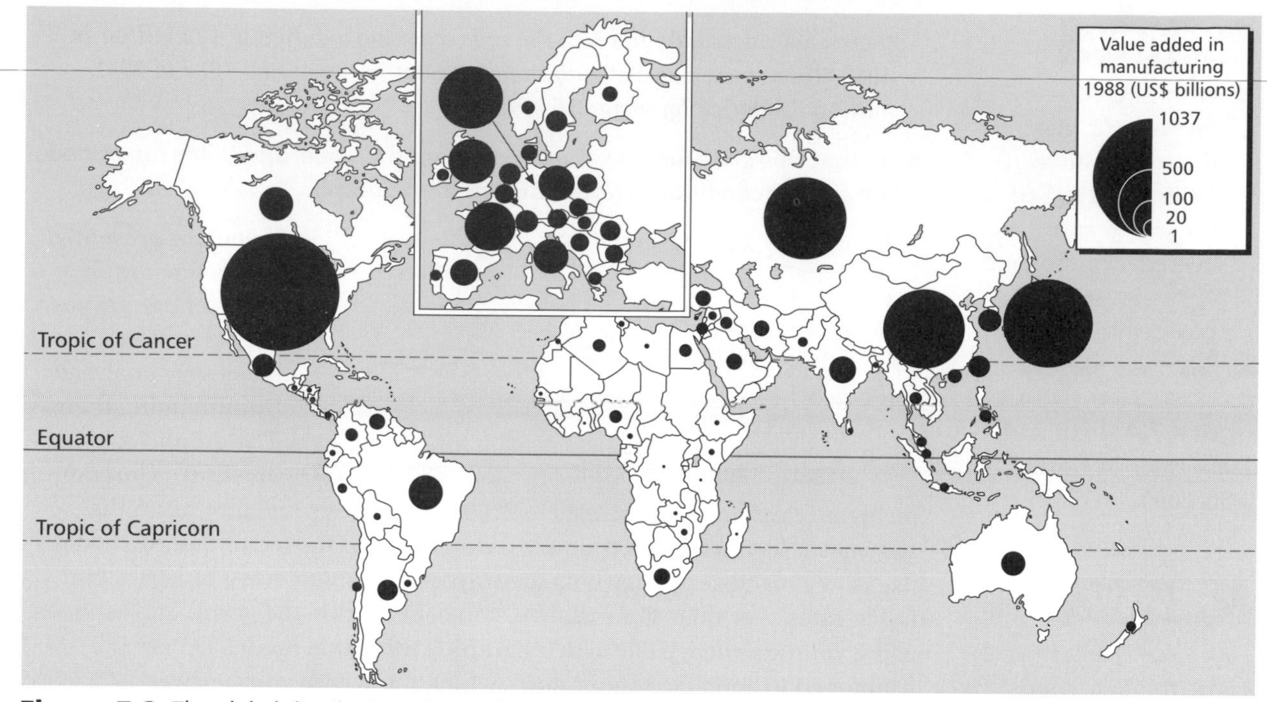

Figure 7.2 The global distribution of manufacturing

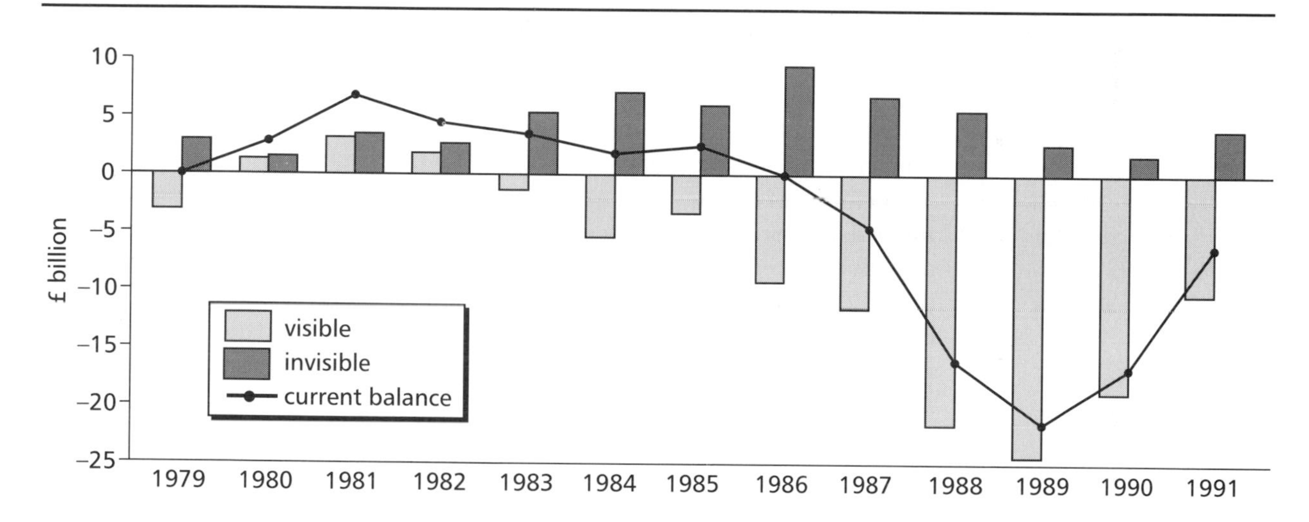

Figure 7.3 The UK's balance of payments, 1979–91

Describing trends over a period of time

You should always try to avoid too detailed a description of changes shown on a graph if you are asked to describe trends over time. Graph **7.3** shows the UK balance of payments, 1979 to 1991. When using composite graphs like this, be sure to make it clear which elements you are describing. If we take the current balance first, this might be described by locating sections where particular trends were similar within the period, but different to those found in periods to either side. For example, the description to go with this graph of current balance might be:

> *Until 1986, the current UK balance of payments was positive (in the black) with 1981 showing the highest surplus of £6 billion. After 1986,*

Review

2 With reference to **7.3** on page 73, describe the trend between 1979 and 1991 of the visible and invisible components of the balance of payments.

there was a dramatic fall into the red, reaching a deficit of £22 billion in 1989. Then there was a steady improvement in the period 1989 to 1991, cutting the deficit by some £15 billion.

Note that this gives actual values read from the scale, and dates for periods when similar conditions were reflected in the graph.

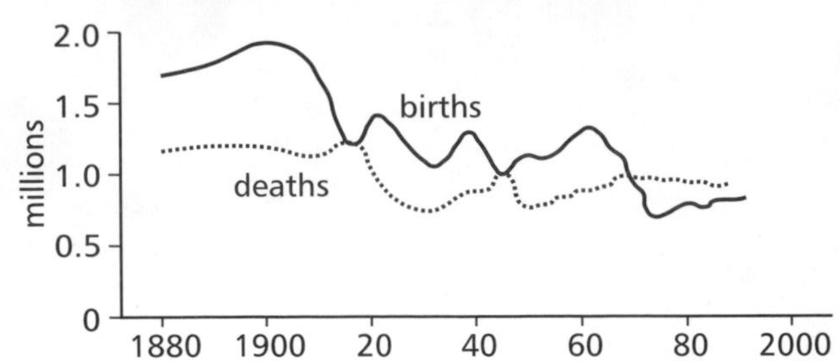

Figure 7.4 Birth and death rates in Germany, 1880–2000

If you are presented with a line graph or a series of bar graphs, they are often effectively analysed by annotating them. The graph **7.4** illustrates German birth and death rates from 1880 to 2000 by using two line graphs on the same axes. Try to avoid too simple a description. One technique you could use is to generalise. This avoids the trap of describing every little rise and fall in rates over time. For instance, you could divide the graph into sections, using your knowledge of the demographic transition model. Do not be frightened to annotate graphs and include them with your answers.

Review

3 Indicate where each of the following labels should be placed in **7.4**:
- standstill
- rapid increase
- slower increase
- natural decrease.

4 Write a short piece of prose describing the trends.

Describing relationships shown on scatter graphs

Three possible correlations on scatter graphs are illustrated in **7.5.** In each case you may need to describe them in correct technical terms and then try to explain why the correlation might occur. Note the titles of the graphs; they give you the correct terms to use. The lines on the graphs show **direct** or **perfect** correlations. The points in A and B suggest that the data **tends towards**, in the first case A a **direct positive correlation** and in B a **direct negative correlation.** The lines simply describe how one factor varies as the other varies. They do not suggest that one changes because the other changes, though you might like to comment on this. For example, in A, if the x axis represented the incidence of sunburn and the y axis represented sales of ice cream, you would see that, as one goes up, so does the other. Nobody in their right mind would suggest that ice cream causes sunburn! The link is temperature. As this rises, both sales of ice cream and cases of sunburn increase. Be careful not to read too much into correlations. All they do is to suggest something else that is worth looking at.

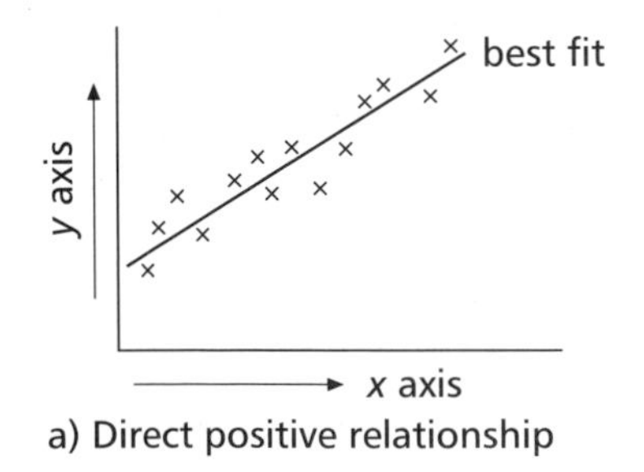

a) Direct positive relationship

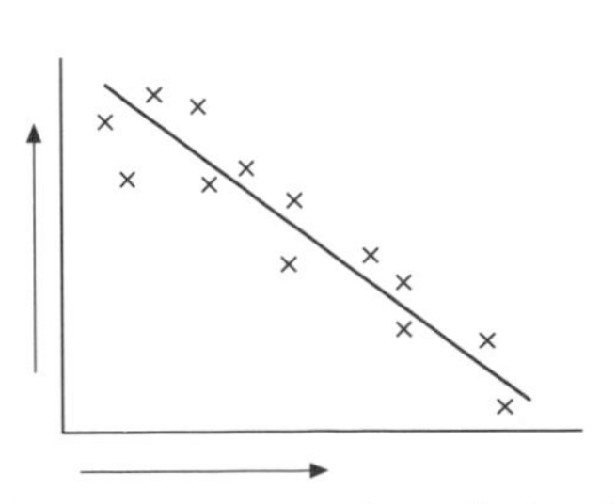

b) Inverse or negative relationship

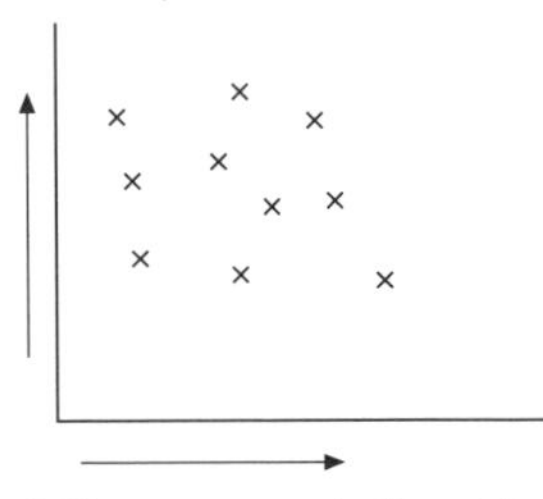

c) No strong relationship evident

Figure 7.5 Describing relationships shown on scatter graphs

Describing relationships shown in proportional graphs

Figure **7.6** shows a series of proportional bar graphs representing the populations of the world's largest cities in 1985 and 2000. The stages required in analysing the pattern in this case are:

- describe the overall trends
- calculate the absolute changes
- calculate the relative changes.

Overall trends You can see that in terms of total growth there is a marked contrast between cities in EMDCs (with little increase) and in ELDCs (all showing signs of quite substantial increase). You could then classify the cities into two major categories, 'fast' and 'slow' growth.

Absolute increase is the number of people expected by 2000. This can be read straight from the scale. For example, Calcutta is forecast to show an absolute increase of some 7 million people.

Relative rates can be established by working out the percentage increases for each city and comparing them. In other words, you will have to spend a little time with a calculator, but it will provide a much better-quality answer once you have done so.

Review

5 Describe the growth of world cities as shown in **7.6** and comment on the trends shown.

In addition to this analysis, you could try ranking the cities in 1985 and in 2000 and comparing them. You could perhaps produce a grid for this to show your working. Figure **7.7** shows a series of proportional bar graphs representing world energy consumption and its sources in 1988, and two possible scenarios of future consumption and supply.

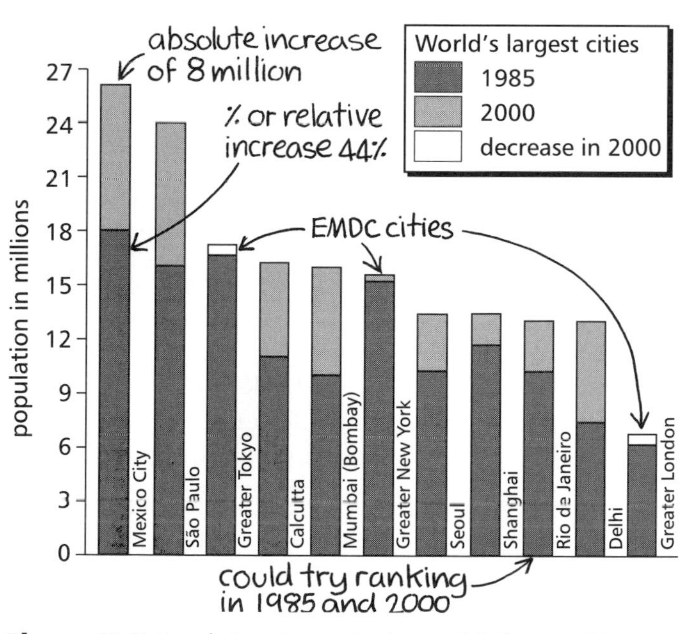

Figure 7.6 Population change in the world's largest cities, 1985 and 2000

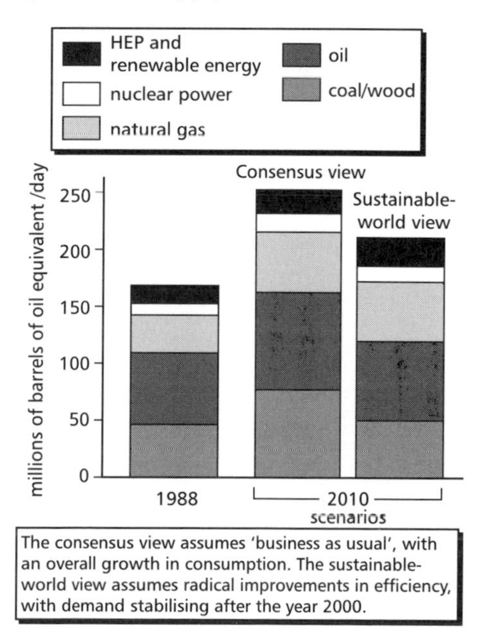

Figure 7.7 Sustainable-world and consensus views of the future energy situation

Review

6 Study 7.7 on page 75. Describe and explain the differences between the two scenarios for 2010. (Don't forget to look at total, absolute and relative amounts in the mix of sources. Be aware of the link between harmful emissions and specific types of fuel.)

7 Now try an open-ended data-response question. Write an analytical account of the information contained in **7.8**.

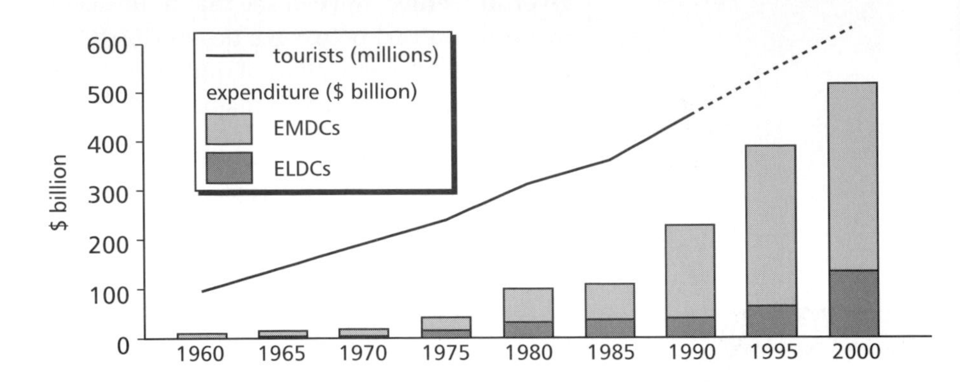

Figure 7.8 Growth in international tourism, 1960–2000

SECTION E

Analysing a photograph or sketch

For both of these, a useful analytical sequence is as follows:

1 Initial preparation, annotating all the key features (using pencil).

2 Establishing a scale for the features in the photograph (area covered, or height, for example).

3 Drawing a grid on the photograph (four quadrants may be enough for you to use to locate the key features).

4 Preparing a structured response plan which links the key features together.

You can try this out with a photograph of an ecosystem (**7.9**). Some key ideas to note include the presence or absence of structure or stratification, a shrub layer, the nature of the ground surface, herb or ground layer, evidence of management and density of vegetation. Try the same technique with photographs in any geography textbook available to you. You should try it on different types of photograph (for example vertical/ oblique aerial photograph, urban/ rural, landscape, etc.) and sketches.

Another useful technique is to produce your own sketch of a photograph. This will enable you to simplify the outline, note the main features and suggest interrelationships. You could rule a box in the centre of your page

Figure 7.9 Photograph of a hot desert landscape

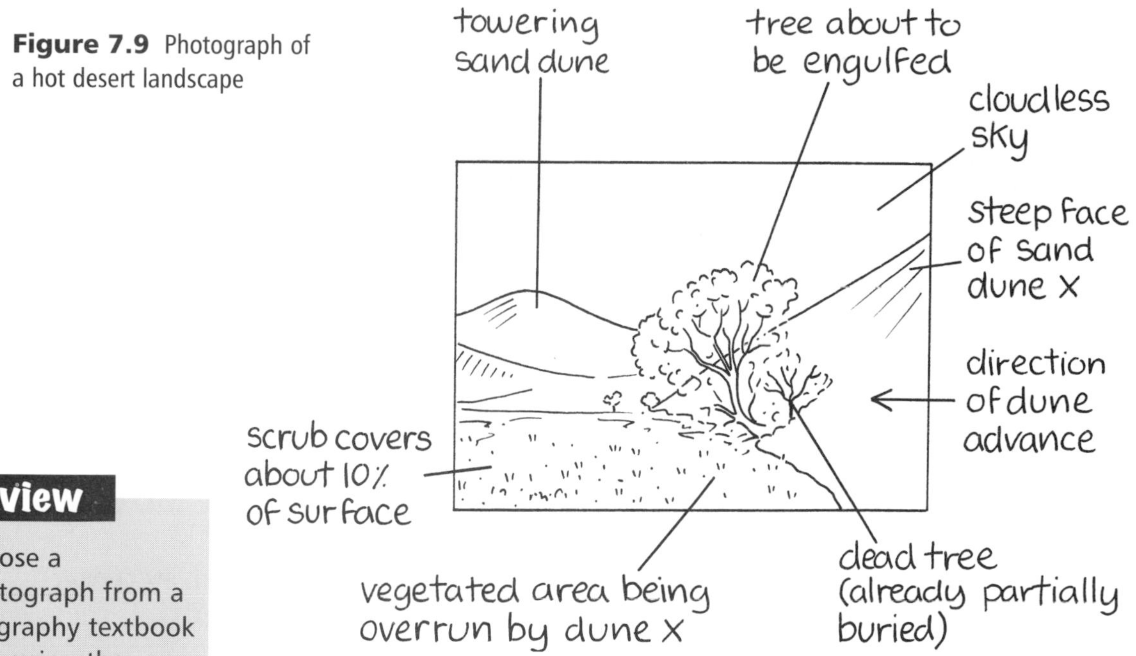

Figure 7.10 An annotated sketch of a hot desert landscape

Review

8 Choose a photograph from a geography textbook and, using the technique described here, produce your own annotated sketch.

and draw a simplified sketch in it. Then draw lines out from the features to the edge of the box, writing explanatory notes outside the sketch. The sketch **7.10** shows an example based on **7.9**.

Analysing statistical tables

This is often seen to be a difficult task, but persistence and a structured approach pay off. The first thing you might do is to annotate the table (**7.11**). Look for trends and groupings of values and mark the key statistics. Highlight the dates of the data.

You may be able to calculate the mean for one set of figures and compare it with that of another set. You might also be able to comment on the variation in any set of figures. It might be possible to draw simple diagrams to convey more clearly the essential character of, or message contained in a set of statistics.

Review

9 Study **7.11** and analyse the main changes in employment taking place between:
a 1981 and 1984 and
b 1984 and 1987.

10 To what extent do the two periods show similar trends?

Category	Employment		
	1987	Net change 1981–84	Net change 1984–87
Primary industry			
Coal mining	39 400	–13 200	–27 500
Other	58 782	–4319	–3382
All primary industry	98 182	–17 519	–30 882
Manufacturing industry			
Mechanical engineering	76 100	–26 200	5700
Food, drink and tobacco	72 100	–12 400	–1500
Textiles	45 900	–10 300	–1200
Manufactured metal goods	37 200	–14 000	4500
Clothing	35 800	–1700	2300
Paper, printing and publishing	35 000	–1200	3400
Metal manufacture	24 600	–16 000	–17 000
Other	155 390	–12 400	1118
All manufacturing industry	482 090	–94 200	–2682
Service industry			
Public administration & defence	284 200	–10 000	20 800
Retail distribution	173 800	–2300	2300
Insurance, banking and finance	128 200	8700	12 500
Other services	127 100	17 800	19 000
Medical services	116 400	11 300	5102
Hotels & catering	89 800	14 500	–2100
Wholesale	81 193	2385	–23
Transport	68 234	–3323	–8675
Other	43 942	5038	–2760
All service industry	1 112 870	44 100	46 142
All employment	**1 693 142**	**–67 619**	**12 578**

latest year
2 periods of change
marked decline
coal mine closure?
all declining 1981-84 but less marked in 1984-87 except metals manufacture which causes an overall decline
employment in these increases
slight increase overall

Figure 7.11 Employment change in the UK, 1981–87

Interpreting a cartoon or advertisement

A cartoon is a very powerful way of presenting a viewpoint. An advertisement nearly always emphasises a particular aspect of the company represented. The first stage in analysing it is to look at the source. This may well reveal the bias. For example, if you look at an advert from British Nuclear Fuels, you would not expect it to mention the potential dangers of nuclear power. Try to develop a critical eye.

In order to analyse a cartoon like the ones in **7.12**, try to identify the following:

- the source of the cartoon
- any bias that may be shown
- the issue or issues being addressed
- the point being made (usually achieved by exaggerating stereotypes)
- your own reactions to the point.

Humour is a very effective way of making a point, but it can also be very dangerous. Unless you are completely confident, do not try to make a joke in your examination answers. But you could easily quote examples of cartoons (and where they appeared) in a question that talks about viewpoints, attitudes or issues. A few cartoons cut out of magazines or newspapers also help to brighten your own notes and may make them more user-friendly.

Review

11 Two cartoons with very different perspectives on aid are reproduced in **7.12**. They were originally published in *New Internationalist*, a magazine with a left-wing bias. Both express a cynical view of different approaches to aid. Analyse the views of aid shown. What sort of aid are they talking about? What arguments for and against aid are illustrated?

Figure 7.12 Different views of aid

Annotating

Some examination questions ask you to annotate a diagram or graph to identify the main features or trends. Figure **7.13** is a block diagram of a coastal area as it appeared in an examination. Candidates were asked to annotate it to show the processes operating (not the features, which were already labelled). Labels should point to the correct spot or area on the diagram. For example, there is no point in labelling the rapid erosion in an

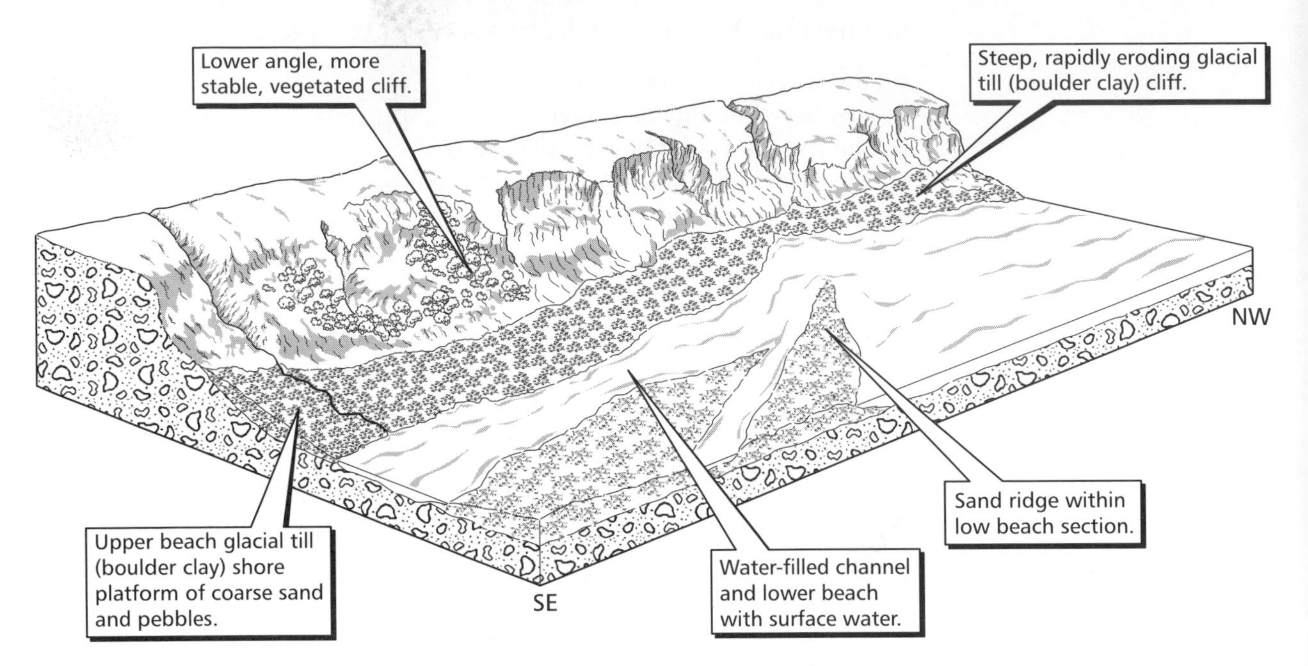

Holderness coast erosion and the significance of ords

The 60km long Holderness coast lies between the chalk promontory of Flamborough Head in the north and the sand and shingle spit of Spurn Head in the south. The coast is backed by Pleistocene glacial till cliffs, renowned for their rapid rate of erosion (approximately 1.2 metres a year).

The most rapid rates of erosion occur at points where there are low sections of beach, which form irregularly along the coast from Barmston in the north to Spurn Head. They are known locally as ords and migrate southwards along this coast. The average rate of movement of the ord is about 0.5km a year but this masks a considerable variation depending on the wind direction and strength. The movement is unpredictable. While the general trend of movement is north to south, there were reversals of this trend.

The undermining of the cliff by wave attack above the cliff foot rapidly produces instability in the unconsolidated glacial till. The partially vegetated cliff, which formed under non-ord conditions, becomes very steep to the point of being almost vertical in some cases.

The rate of erosion from the cliffs is such that the ord clearly contributes to the budget of materials on the beaches of Holderness and the spit at the mouth of the Humber. It has been calculated that half a million cubic metres of cliff have been removed in some years but in all cases the rate of removal is greater in the winter months. The ord cliffs were eroded four times more heavily than the inter-ord cliffs between 1974 and 1982. Cliff-top recession was marked, averaging 0.7m in the summer months and 3.4m in the winter.

Figure 7.13
An annotated block diagram of a coast

area that has been subsequently covered with vegetation. The labels must contain a good amount of detail, including technical information, to demonstrate that you understand what is going on, but you should keep each label concise (up to 10 words apiece). You might also add extra information to this particular diagram to explain, for example, how the factors (geology, slope, lubrication, etc.) affect the process.

Figure 7.14 Features produced by periglacial processes

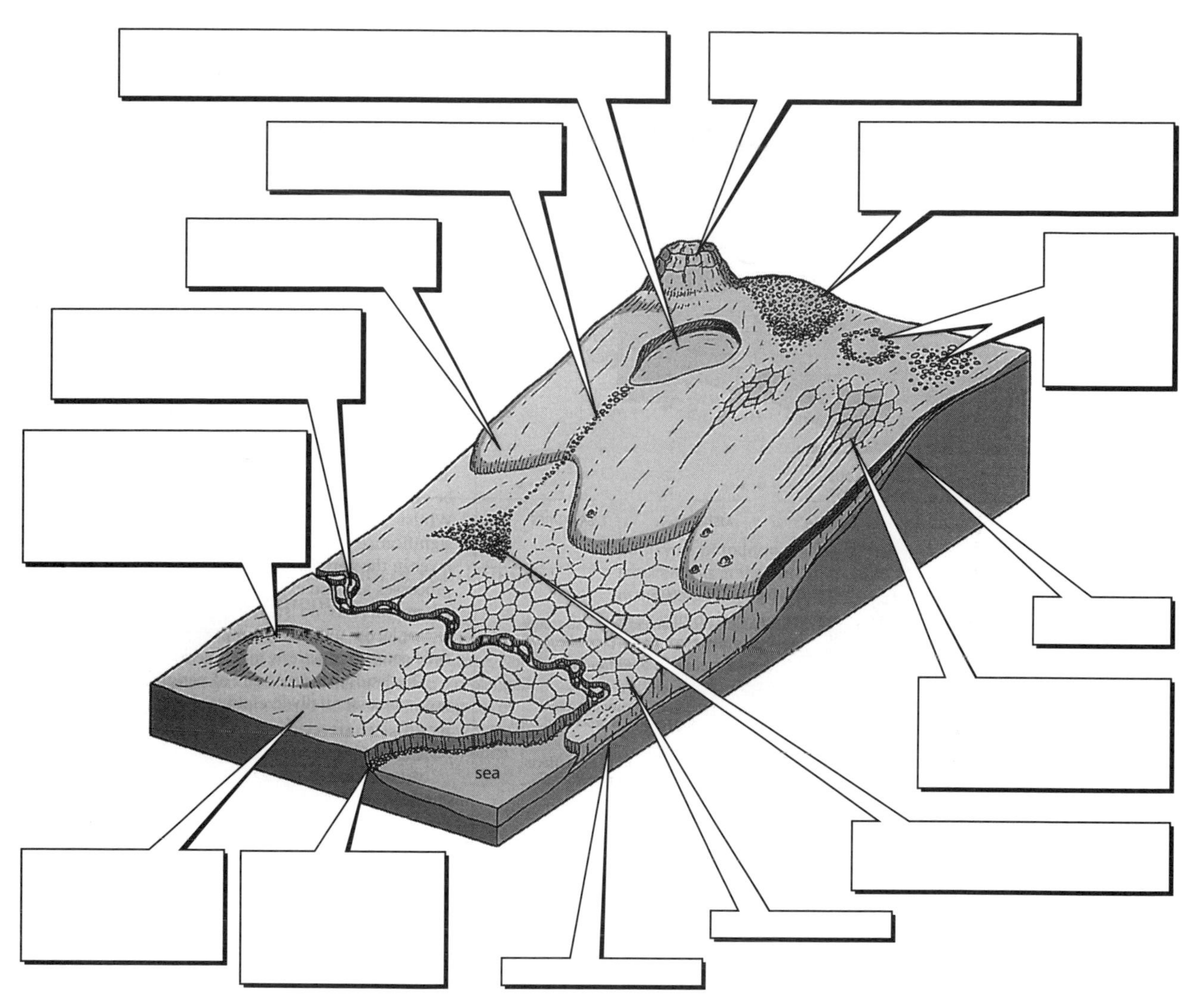

Review

12 Diagram **7.14** shows the characteristic features of a periglacial landscape. Copy and then annotate the diagram by identifying the features and in each label writing a sentence about the origins of the feature.

Try this one

Prepare an answer to the structured question opposite, following advice already given in Section B:

- Read the question carefully, paying proper attention to the maps (and their keys) and the statistics.
- Obey the command words.
- Be precise – make proper use of geographical terminology.
- Keep to the point; don't waste time and effort repeating the question.
- Check your answers. Have you paid sufficient attention to the stimulus material?

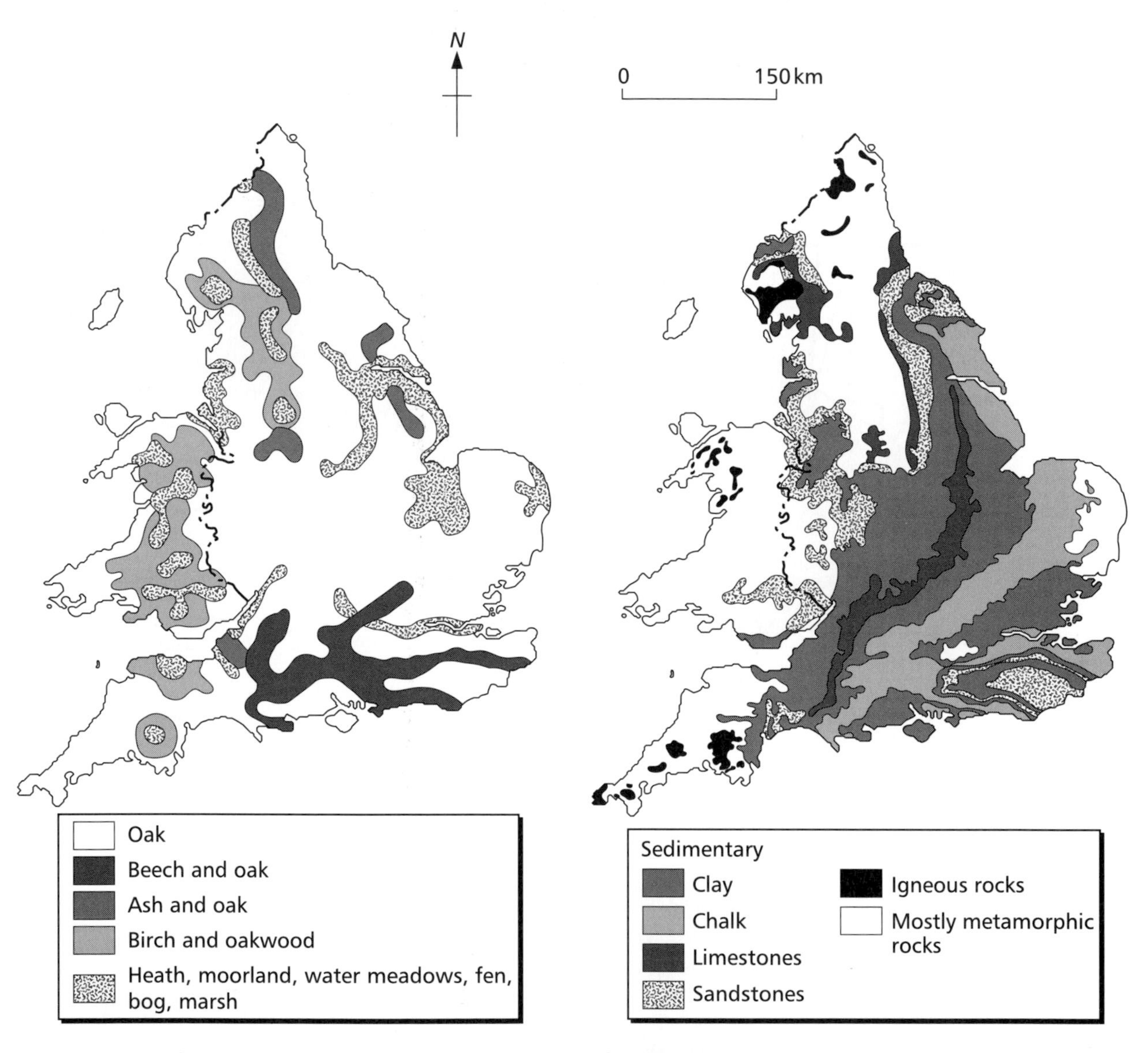

Figure 7.15 The distribution of natural vegetation in England and Wales

Figure 7.16 Simplified geological map of England and Wales

Figure 7.17 Woodland changes in England and Wales, 1947–2000 (thousand ha)

Year	Broad-leaved woodland	Mixed woodland	Coniferous
1947	851	106	104
1969	712	149	329
2000 (est.)	483	102	634

a Describe the distribution of beech and oak forests in England and Wales. (3 marks)

b **i)** State the relationship between geology and the distribution you have described in (**a**). (2 marks)

ii) Suggest reasons for the relationship. (4 marks)

c **i)** Identify the main changes that have occurred since 1947 in the stock and character of British woodland. (4 marks)

ii) Explain the changes you have identified in (**i**). (4 marks)

d List ways in which woodland in the UK is under pressure from other land uses. (4 marks)

e Give examples of actions that have been taken to reduce the pressure. (4 marks)

CHAPTER

8

Preparing for decision-making exercises

Many A-level Geography syllabuses now contain a decision-making exercise as part of the examination. Check to see whether this is the case for your syllabus. If it does, you should find this chapter particularly useful. With the exception of the Northern Ireland Examination Board, all the other GCE Boards setting a decision-making question send out their resources approximately two weeks before the examination. Getting ready for this examination component will, therefore, involve two phases:

1 Long-term preparation, gradually building up the requisite skills.

2 Final preparation – when the resources have arrived.

SECTION A

Long-term preparation

There are three main aspects to this. First, there are **generic skills** such as interpreting Ordnance Survey maps, aerial photographs and satellite images. Secondly there are specific **decision-making skills**. A very useful book to use in developing these skills is K. A. Cowlard, *Decision-making in Geography* (Hodder & Stoughton, 1990). This shows you exactly how to set about designing a table (tabulation), scaling data, developing techniques to compare options (matrixes) and ranking things in order according to a specified criterion (**8.1**). Some of these skills were touched on in **Chapter 7**.

Figure 8.1 A summary of techniques for decision-making exercises

Name of technique	Description of technique	Suitability/Use of technique	Points to watch
TABULATION	Provides a summarised visual display to highlight key issues of a complex situation.	Can be used to clarify the main issues because it concentrates on essentials.	Can tend towards brevity. Not a good way of evaluation or providing detailed explanation. Make sure it saves time.
SCALING	Provides a means of relative positioning of often qualitative data, to allow comparison and analysis. Chosen scales can of course be weighted.	• *Ordinal*, e.g. 1 = low priority → 4 = high priority. • *Bipolar*, e.g. 2 = negative 0 = neutral +2 = positive. • *Profile chart* showing scaling visually. • *Forcefield* shows strengths or pros and cons (1 →10) visually.	Involves personal subjective ranking so may introduce bias, especially where users are inexperienced.

Name of technique	Description of technique	Suitability/Use of technique	Points to watch
MATRICES	Provides a multi-dimensional diagram in grid form to show relationships between individual variables.	Useful in a wide variety of contexts to summarise large sets of data in figure, rank and form. • { *Checklist matrix.* / *Summary matrix.* } • *Compatibility/conflict matrix* for analysing values. • *Evaluation matrices* in weighted or scaled form. • *Priority matrix* for options. • *Environmental impact matrix.*	May need annotation and explanation, especially for an evaluation exercise Usually concentrates on negative impacts.
RANKING	Provides a means of ordering schemes in order to identify priorities.	Criteria can be individually scaled, weighted, and then ranked. A composite or an average rank can be generated.	Correct selection of criteria. Need to provide evidence. Quantitative data is more manageable than qualitative.
DECISION-MAKING PLANS	Provides a logical approach to decision-making processes.	• *Decision tree* charts a sequence of decisions over time. • *Analysis of interconnected decision areas* (AIDA) using strategy diagrams. • *Critical path analysis* to schedule a sequence. • *Cost-benefit analysis.*	Only useful for outline planning. Can be simplistic. Relies on detailed financial and statistical data.

The third strand to the long-term preparation is discovering the **specific requirements** of your particular examination board. In particular you need to find out what part of the syllabus it can be set on, how long you will get to do the task, and so on. For example, if you are studying ULEAC Syllabus B, your decision-making exercise has a synoptic function. The aim is to draw together your knowledge, understanding and skills. This is achieved by asking you to research a topic that reaches across the Physical Environment and Human Environment modules. You have $2\frac{1}{4}$ hours to complete the task.

A good way to succeed in the long term is to get as much practice as you can. At frequent intervals, tackle the tasks set in previous papers and look at examiners' reports and mark schemes to check whether you got them right.

SECTION B

Short-term preparation

The concept of take-away resources is comparatively recent (NEAB pioneered the style in 1995). Since then it has been discovered that there is a real danger of candidates over-preparing. This, in turn, takes away from revision time for other parts of the examination and other subjects.

About 5 hours' preparation time should be sufficient for this task. Whatever you do, even if the location described in the materials in very close to where you live, do not go and visit the site. Quite probably, the exercise has been heavily adapted. Do not consider ringing up the Planning Office either. Too much information can be dangerous. Remember, you are only being tested on what you can analyse from the resources supplied and at their face value. You should not put yourself in the position of reading things into the materials that you cannot deduce from the evidence they contain.

In some cases, such as the ULEAC Syllabus B, your teacher is allowed to have a discussion session with you when the resources arrive. This will be very helpful in focusing your preparation, for example picking out the salient points of any statistics, etc. The next two sections in this chapter are clearly appropriate for this session.

SECTION C

Identifying the requisite terms and techniques

The nature of the resources will tell you exactly what topic the exercise is going to focus on. Clearly, if all the data relate to flooding, then you need to spend a good hour reading through your notes on this specific subject to make sure you understand all the technical concepts, such as **recurrence interval**, **lag time**, **urbanisation** and **catchment**.

Another clue to the knowledge and understanding required may lie in the resources and the techniques used. If you see some results from **statistical** analyses (e.g. Rs = 0.87) and there are 15 items listed in the data with their ranks compared, you will need to look up your notes on Spearman's rank correlation and make sure you understand all about the **null hypothesis**, **critical values**, etc. Equally, if you have some results of a questionnaire survey in the resources it may be very useful to look up your notes on **sampling** including possible methods, together with the concept of **sampling error**.

You also need to revise all your decision-making techniques. More about this later.

SECTION D

Checking out the resources

It is absolutely vital to spend some time working on the resources themselves. There are a number of steps you can take to ensure that you are well prepared.

1 Interpreting all the graphs, statistics and tables

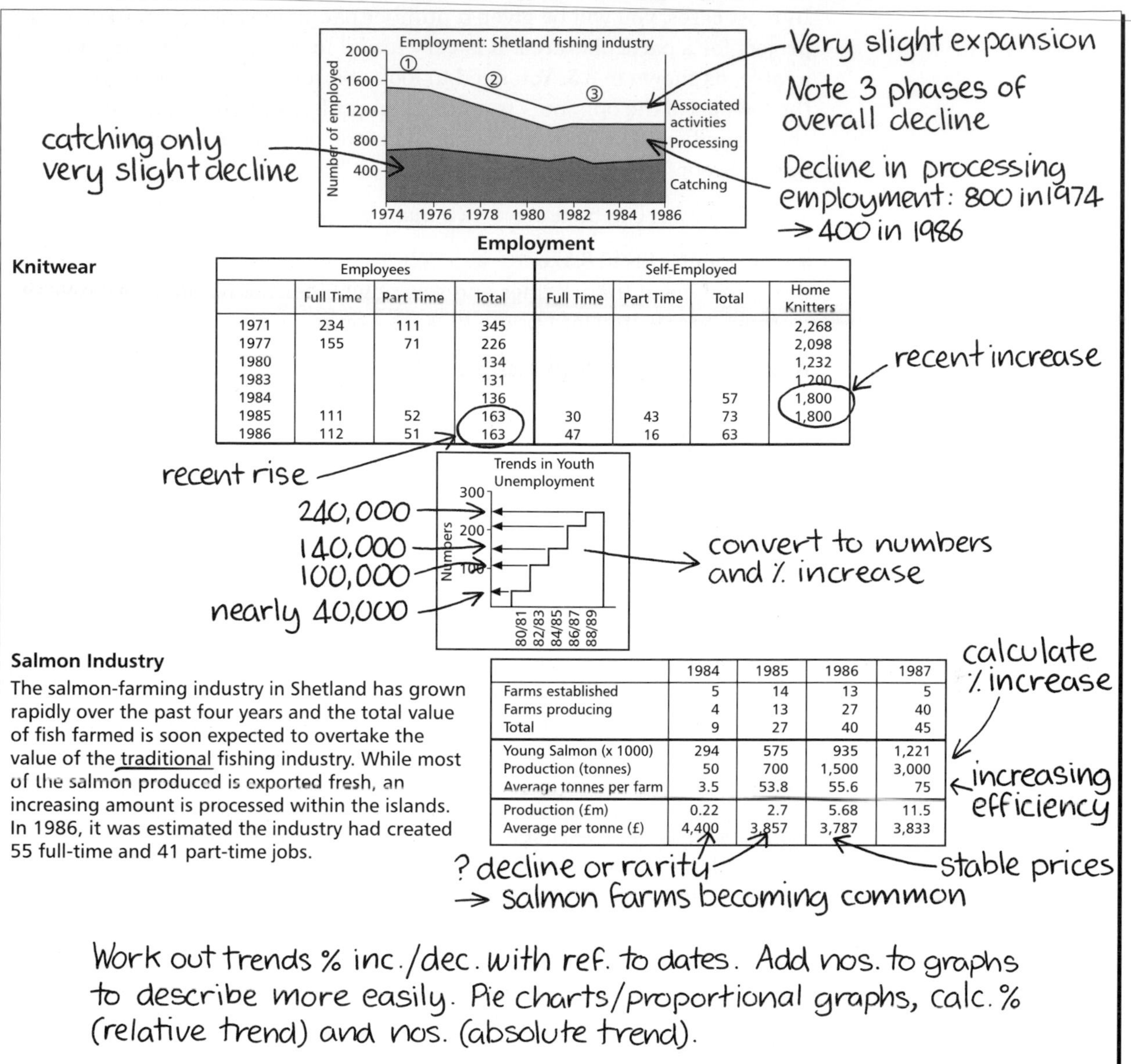

Knitwear

Employment

	Employees			Self-Employed			
	Full Time	Part Time	Total	Full Time	Part Time	Total	Home Knitters
1971	234	111	345				2,268
1977	155	71	226				2,098
1980			134				1,232
1983			131				1,200
1984			136			57	1,800
1985	111	52	163	30	43	73	1,800
1986	112	51	163	47	16	63	

Salmon Industry

The salmon-farming industry in Shetland has grown rapidly over the past four years and the total value of fish farmed is soon expected to overtake the value of the traditional fishing industry. While most of the salmon produced is exported fresh, an increasing amount is processed within the islands. In 1986, it was estimated the industry had created 55 full-time and 41 part-time jobs.

	1984	1985	1986	1987
Farms established	5	14	13	5
Farms producing	4	13	27	40
Total	9	27	40	45
Young Salmon (x 1000)	294	575	935	1,221
Production (tonnes)	50	700	1,500	3,000
Average tonnes per farm	3.5	53.8	55.6	75
Production (£m)	0.22	2.7	5.68	11.5
Average per tonne (£)	4,400	3,857	3,787	3,833

Figure 8.2 Interpreting graphs, statistics and tables

Figure **8.2** shows a selection of graphs and tables annotated by a student as part of their preparation. The materials are from the ULEAC 1989 Shetland Islands decision-making exercise.

2 Working through map extracts and photographs

It is particularly useful if you are given a map and an aerial photograph to match them and annotate both resources to build up a detailed mental picture of the area. You might identify:

- relief features, e.g. scarp slopes, plateaux or coastal features
- drainage features, e.g. floodplain features, drainage patterns, etc.
- urban features, such as functional zones, the age/nature of housing, etc.

3 Analysing opinions and values

In most cases, you will be given a number of opinions about an issue or a project for a particular area. It is very useful to check these out and devise a table, as shown in **8.3**. You need to look at issues such as the 'standing' of the 'owner' of the opinion – is it based on professional research, fact, or sheer emotion? Do the resources support the opinion in any way? Do the opinions conflict with each other?

Values analysis can be done in two main ways:

- by opinion (as in **8.3**) or
- by looking at the schemes and seeing whether the opinions approve of them, are neutral, or oppose them (**8.4** on page 90).

As you can see from **8.3b**, it is possible to build up a matrix. This resource is again based on the ULEAC 1989 Shetland Islands decision-making exercise.

4 Looking at options (such as a choice between 6 schemes, 3 sites, etc.)

Whilst it is obviously not a good idea to prejudge the question, it is nevertheless highly likely that you will have to compare the options in one way or another. This might involve looking at advantages and disadvantages, socio-economic benefits and negative impacts or straightforward cost-benefit analysis. It is therefore advantageous to spend time looking at the schemes and preparing a revision table to summarise information from all sources about them.

Figure **8.4a** shows five schemes proposed for the economic development of the Shetland Islands, and in **8.4b** the student has prepared a table that compares them in a number of ways. Note that if you use summary tables, ideally they should be on a large sheet of paper to allow for bullet-point summaries to show really detailed information. This should persuade the examiner that you are worth considering for maximum marks. It is absolutely no use at all merely lifting information and evidence from the resource. At A-level you have to interpret it just as the student has done in **8.4b**.

You will also need to revise all your decision-making skills, in particular (amongst a wide range of techniques) the procedures for constructing effective **matrixes**, carrying out **scaling** exercises and **bi-polar analysis**. Figure **8.5** on page 91 summarises the process of deciding on and using an effective analysis procedure.

a)

Representative statements

1 'Anything that will bring a better price for our fish is welcome. Do you know that some of our catch sells for as little as 4p a pound to the Klondiker ships and that influences the price for other wholesalers? It makes you wonder how fish gets to be so expensive in the supermarkets!'

Whalsay fisherman

2 'I think that the new recreation complex is a great idea. There's not much to do here but it's a pity that it is to be on the west coast; it would be better in Lerwick.'

Youth in Lerwick

3 'These are an interesting set of proposals. I can't say that I think much of the proposed recreation complex – not of much interest to the type of tourist we get here; in fact, it might damage tourism. The more we can do for the woollen industry the better. That's the sort of thing people want to come and see and buy. The new airport? Well, it's very convenient, but then the old airport was only an hour away from Lerwick and, of course, there was little overflying the land.'

Spokesperson for the Shetland Hoteliers

4 'I see great problems with the salmon farming. It's a bit of an eyesore. There's plenty of salmon farms in Scotland and there seems to be the threat of disease. As for the hotel, I just can't believe that permission would be given to site it near the old abbey where all that famous silver treasure was found, and what is going to become of that famous tombolo?'

John Roberts, Scottish Heritage Council

5 'So many of the proposals are set in Lerwick! It's very hard to find good housing there anyway; there is little to rent and the prices are high. As for the noise and disturbance that will come with these proposals – well, one did leave London to enjoy the peace and the solitude!'

Cynthia Clogston-Wilmott, Voluntary Worker for the Donaldson Housing Trust

6 'Transport and communications – that's the key to successful development. It would not matter where any proposal was sited if travel was easy and quick. Mind you, some of the tourists seem to like the narrow roads and the isolation they create.'

Arthur Ronaldson, resident of Hillswick

b)

Opinion number	Scheme	Summary of views	For or neutral, against	Evidence for views	Conflicts with	Status of opinion
1	Fish factory	Need for (AFP) where fish made into high-value convenience foods for more profit, increased markets. Only basic FP on island	For: fish factory will increase value of products to compete with Klondikers	Only advanced plant on islands. Fish is sold very cheaply to foreign-owned Klondikers. Essentially true	? Residents of Lerwick, who will smell the factory	Directly or emotionally involved. Fisherman knows industry. Solid status?
2	Recreation complex	In agreement with idea but wants it in Lerwick	For: but not on west coast	Photo evidence showing remoteness and beauty of Ninians some miles from centres of population	Concept of tourism complex. Youth wants complex for locals	Just a personal opinion about facilities of Lerwick. Low status?

Figure 8.3 Analysing opinions

a)

PROPOSED FIVE PROJECTS TO ENCOURAGE DEVELOPMENT IN THE SHETLAND ISLANDS

1 Salmon Farming (SF)

The Council will establish salmon farms at the five sites show on Enclosure 7. The farms, which will be owned by individuals or co-operatives, will be purchased by a low-interest loan that will be repaid over a ten-year period. Expected employment is about 7 people per site. Expected cost of construction is about £1.3 million.

2 Advanced Fish-Processing (FPM)

At present there are several basic fish-processing plants on the islands. At these plants, the fish are gutted, skinned, cleaned, frozen and, sometimes, market-packaged. The Council proposes to establish a factory to part-cook and package fish for convenience foods. This would be expected to command a better price and a wider market. It would be sited in Lerwick and initially would employ 28 people. Expected cost of construction is £2.2 million.

3 Hotel Complex (HC)

The creation of a hotel complex on, or adjacent to, St Ninian's Isle is proposed. The complex would have chalet and hotel accommodation, together with extensive recreational facilities such as an indoor pool, skating rink and disco. This might prove an attraction for visitors and encourage additional holiday-makers. This would employ 140 people but the jobs would be part-time and mainly female. Expected costs to the Islands are estimated to be £12 million.

4 Support for the Knitwear Industry (KF and KM)

The reputation of Shetland wool and the attractiveness of the unique Shetland designs have encouraged firms from all over the world to use the name Shetland in order to sell their own garments. The Council will establish a factory in Walls to dye the wool. The wool is at present sent to the Scottish mainland to be dyed. In addition, a marketing and distribution group will be created near Lerwick to support the recently created Shetland Knitwear Traders' Association. This will provide advertising for the product and the new certified Shetland trade mark. This would employ 9 people in Walls and 2 in Lerwick. Expected construction costs are £300 000.

5 Improved communications

The existing main airport is sited at the extreme southern end of the island, largely for historical reasons. It is proposed to resite the main airport at a more central location. In addition, all the single-track roads would be upgraded to allow traffic to travel in each direction at the same time. This would reduce by 30%, in broad terms, the car-travel times given in Enclosure 5. Bus services are extremely infrequent, e.g. two or three buses per week. Despite the expected EU aid in support of this infrastructure project, there is no doubt that the costs to the islands would still be considerable. The project could employ 400 people for 6 years but thereafter only 5 additional jobs will be provided. Estimated costs to the Islands are £19 million.

b)

Number	Location	Cost	Employment	Ownership	Ease of development
1	5 sites across islands not Lerwick	Construction £1.3 million	7 at 5 sites = (35) Cost per job £37,000+	Individuals/ co-operatives. 10yr low interest	Could start immediatley. ? planning permission
2	In Lerwick	Construction £2.2 million	Directly (28) Cost per job £78,571 but supporting 600 fishermen	Council owned	Issues of planning permission in Lerwick
3	In remote St. Ninians Isle	£12 million	Part-time female jobs = 70 ft equiv.	Not known	Would expect NIMBY revolt ∵ of quality of environment

Number	Environmental impacts	+ and	−
1	In sheltered fjords (see photo) Visual? Sedimentation. Disease issues (Fig 3)	? Outside Lerwick. Housing issues, etc. Good money spinner (see salmon stats)	Problems of environment
2	Smell, fish guts, extra traffic noise	Adding value to an industry on hard times. Wider markets	Problems of location in Lerwick, already overheating → housing problems
3			

Figure 8.4 Weighing up options

Figure 8.5 The effective use of matrices

- Establish the criteria from the question.
- Draft out the framework.
- Insert all the evidence from the materials.
- Decide on the **nature** of the scale. You can use ordinal scales (e.g. +1, +2, +3, etc.) for impacts or bi-polar scales (e.g. –2 to +2) for any exercise that looks at costs and benefits, advantages or disadvantages. The **magnitude** is also important. If you use only a narrow range, such –1 to +1, it is unlikely to differentiate, but if you go as far as –10 to +10 you have to be very sure of your evidence, as it is difficult to decide subjectively between values in such a wide range.
- Consider whether or not to 'weight' any of the criteria. For example, if you think that climate is twice as important as vegetation cover in determining the propensity of an area to flood, you need to introduce a factor of x2 when awarding the points for this factor.
- Write an explanatory note explaining the scaling technique used and the need for any weighting.

You may then have to go on to rank the options. In this case, you can use a table which values schemes directly by criteria and then comes to a final ranking. You can miss out the scaling stage and go straight for a ranking system, but it must be based on the evidence in front of you.

Often when you have done the ranking, you do have to justify the best option (just one) or the ordering of your ranking (all). You need to be very careful here and remind yourself that you do have to say why you made the choice and why you did not select others, or found them less favourable. This is known as the **rejection factor**.

SECTION E

Final revision

You will not be able to take your annotated resources into the examination room. So you should take a last look through all of your preparatory work shortly before sitting the examination.

Whilst you are tackling the decision-making exercise remember the acronym **CRESTT**.

***C*omprehensiveness** – make sure you cover all the required angles.

***R*ubric** – make sure you do as asked by the command words (e.g. describe, analyse, summarise, etc.) and the questions. A major problem in a take-away exercise is that you may have tried to guess the question and got it wrong.

***E*vidence** – always quote and interpret evidence to support your answer **not** just by saying something like 'e.g. item 7' but 'as shown by the 127% increase in …'.

***S*tructure** – follow a logical route through your enquiry.

***T*iming** – look at the mark allocation and make out a schedule as soon as you see the paper.

***T*echniques** – do not go over the top. If you are asked for **a** technique, you must use only **one**. If the techniques to be used are not specified, weigh up the time factor and the advantages that might be gained from including extra analysis – the latter might be minimal.

Apply the advice embodied in this acronym and you will be riding the CRESTT of a wave when you have completed the examination paper!

SECTION F

Try this one

In order for you to try out some decision-making skills, an exercise on global warming is provided here.

Background

Although scientific research is on-going, most researchers would agree that global warming is indeed occurring, with evidence of significant worldwide temperature rises over the last 30 years. What they disagree about is whether this is a natural process or an enhanced effect brought about by the emission of quantities of greenhouse gases largely generated by the burning of fossil fuels.

The Kyoto Summit Conference (1997) was concerned with the complex issues of atmospheric pollution. All the nations represented at the Conference agreed on targets for emission control. However, in reaching this agreement, tensions were exposed between the so-called 'green' nations and those, such as the USA, where political pressures are very strong for the 'business as usual' scenario. Tensions were also revealed between the EMDCs on the one hand and the NICs and ELDCs on the other. The latter group comprise those countries currently undergoing, or eagerly anticipating, rapid economic development. Is it reasonable to expect them to curb their hopes by asking them to cut back on their consumption of fossil fuels?

The exercise

This involves three documents, **8.6–8.8**.

Item **8.6** is a commissioning letter that sets the scene for the final report.

Figure 8.6
Commissioning letter

Dear Algy

We are pleased to welcome you to the United Nations Panel on Global Atmospheric Research.

Before we commission any new investigations, it is important that we assess the present situation and evaluate current research on global warming, particularly on the alleged part played by rising levels of CO_2 in the atmosphere. Please begin your survey by referring to published materials (articles, books, etc.) in the Library and on CD-ROMs.

Please remember that, just as in a court of law, a pollutant is normally regarded as innocent until proven guilty. It is vital that you weigh up the evidence both for and against the allegation that rising CO_2 levels in the atmosphere are causing global warming. Possibly you may regard the potential impacts of global warming to be so serious that you recommend action even though we may lack complete proof as to the impact of CO_2 emissions.

You need to be aware that different groups and nations have vested interests and therefore strikingly contrasting views on the issue. Try to identify and explain those conflicting approaches.

Currently, expert opinion seems to have arrived at a number of possible ways of reducing the so-called 'greenhouse effect'. We need you to assess the likely social, economic and environmental impacts of those proposed ways.

Finally, in the light of your findings, we would like you to recommend a strategy that the United Nations might endorse. You must be able to justify your recommendation, explaining why you opted for this particular one and rejected the others.

I wish you every success in reaching a sound conclusion and I look forward to reading your report.

Yours sincerely

Chairman
UN Panel on Global Atmospheric Research

People's Republic of China
The greenhouse effect is a plot by the developed world to slow down the rate of development outside the First World. If the rich countries are serious about dealing with the problem then they must be prepared to put up the money to allow us to develop alternative energy strategies.

Organisation of Petroleum Exporting Countries (OPEC)
We do not accept that there is a serious risks of global warming occurring. We call for more research before the world curbs the use of fossil fuels. In the meantime, we propose to fund a body to research into ways of lowering levels of CO_2 in the atmosphere. We are aware that the Japanese are already engaged in research into ways of reducing emissions and we would also support research into the synthesis of chlorophyll.

Republican Party, USA
We regard the global warming scare as a load of baloney. It is a plot by the green movement to undermine capitalism. We should carry on as before and make the USA and the rest of the world a richer place.

Federation of Indian Ocean Islands
We believe that global warming must be taken seriously because all of our islands lie only a few metres above sea-level. If sea-level rose significantly we would literally disappear. We are calling on the rest of the world to sacrifice economic growth to save our islands.

Nuclear power lobby
Fossil fuels can cause all manner of pollution. CO_2 is just one of them. Safe nuclear energy is the long-term answer to the problem. It means that the world does not have to sacrifice economic growth for a stable climate.

The Green Movement
All the nations of the world must set aside self-interest and work together to make the world safe for the 21st century. Even though we cannot predict the future with absolute certainty, recent models of the atmosphere are now much more sophisticated and we can be more confident in them. We cannot risk the possible outcomes of global warming by a reckless pursuit of economic development around the world.

Figure 8.7 Conflicting attitudes about global warming

1 The technological fix
Scientists can solve the potential problems of global warming. Atmospheric CO_2 levels could be reduced by pumping CO_2 directly into the oceans where it would be taken up by plankton, eventually forming limestone (a long-term store for carbon). The oceanic absorption of CO_2 could be further aided by broadcasting iron filings into the sea. Since iron is the nutrient in short supply in sea-water, this would increase plankton growth and therefore increase the uptake of CO_2.

It should also be possible to reduce the amount of incoming solar radiation. Injecting SO_2 into the upper atmosphere would lead to the formation of sulphate aerosols that reflect the sun's rays back into space. We know that this would occur, because after volcanic eruptions, such as Mount Pinatubo, the increase in global SO_2 has led to short-term cooling. It may also be possible to reduce incoming radiation by blasting dust into the upper atmosphere using conventional missile technology.

2 Reducing CO_2 emissions
The only sure way to avoid the risk of global warming is to achieve a worldwide reduction in CO_2 levels. This can be achieved by all countries agreeing to reduce the use of fossil fuels. The wealthy developed countries will need to give serious financial and technological aid to the poorer countries. Reduced emissions can be achieved by a combination of alternative energy, promotion of public transport and energy efficiency, taxation of fossil fuel use and an acceptance that not all economic and social problems can be solved through economic development and increased consumption. The global economy will have to stabilise and the rich countries accept a lowering of their material standards of living. All countries must make cuts – the unilateral action of one country would be completely ineffectual.

3 Carry on as we are
The reduction in the use of fossil fuels would lead to a massive global recession and greatly increase suffering in the less-developed countries. It would be impossible to get all countries to agree to make reductions anyway. Models used to predict climatic change are notoriously unreliable, so why sacrifice global standards of living on the basis of an unproved scientific theory?

4 Plant more trees
The solution is simple – plant more trees. The trees will lock up CO_2 and reduce levels in the atmosphere. Even if the trees are subsequently used for power generation, the next crop of trees would absorb the CO_2 released. Power companies in the West that wish to burn fossil fuels should be obliged to contribute to afforestation projects in tropical countries. Even in developed countries more trees should be planted.

Figure 8.8 Alternative strategies for dealing with global warming

Your final report should cover the following aspects; mark allocations are indicated.

1. An evaluation of published data to determine the extent of global warming and the change in CO_2 levels. (10 marks)
2. An explanation of the greenhouse effect, using an annotated diagram. (10 marks)
3. Consideration of the conflicting attitudes towards the greenhouse effect (**8.7**). (15 marks)
4. Evaluation of the four options put forward to deal with the problem of global warming (**8.8**). (20 marks)
5. A concluding statement recommending and justifying either one of the four strategies or your own alternative. The last could be a combination of strategies.

Further instructions

As a preparation for the exercise, you need to read up about the issues. *The Times* CD-ROM or the Internet will provide a wealth of data, as well as the standard textbooks on environmental pollution and weather and climate.

The exercise should take about 2 hours to write once you have done the research. Follow all the rules, such as timing each part with reference to mark weightings, making sure you have a clear and sound structure for the report, and above all quoting supporting evidence. You could also produce a matrix in which you match the conflicting attitudes of the six parties to the four alternatives on offer. You can use either symbols (agree ✓, neutral *O*, disagree ✗) or some form of points score from +2 strongly agree through to –2 strongly disagree.

When you write your concluding statement, don't forget that the required justification includes not only a strong piece of writing in favour of the chosen option or strategy, but also a brief paragraph explaining why other options were rejected.

CHAPTER

9 The personal enquiry

SECTION A

Introduction

All A-level Geogaphy syllabuses today require you to undertake and submit a personal enquiry. The actual title given to this requirement of the Common Core in Geography varies from one GCE board to another. 'Individual enquiry', 'Individual study', 'Geographical investigation' and 'Personal investigation' are just some of them.

It is stipulated that the personal enquiry should be based on primary data that you have collected, in most cases through fieldwork. You are also encouraged to make use of relevant secondary data (i.e. published material or data collected by someone else to which you refer). The enquiry is an important opportunity for you to work as an individual outside the pressures of the exam room, and to demonstrate your knowledge and understanding, but most important of all your command of geographical skills.

The topic and methods chosen may have to be approved by an external moderator. Your study should have a very clear focus, defined as a question, issue, problem or hypothesis that is within the syllabus. Although the enquiry is first marked by your teachers, a process of moderation subsequently takes place to ensure that all teachers have marked to the same standards.

The personal enquiry is a major component of the A-level examination. Its weighting in the overall assessment is between 15 and 20 per cent of the total marks. The figure varies from board to board, just as does the word limit imposed on the final report of the investigation. The limit usually lies in the range of 2500–5000 words. It is vital that you find out the precise word limit set by your board. Be sure that you do not exceed it.

SECTION B

What's it all about?

In order to give you some 'feel' as to the nature and aims of the personal enquiry it might be helpful to make you aware of the possible criteria that will be used in the assessment of your final report. Clearly, the exact criteria and their relative weighting vary from board to board, but are likely to include some of the following:

- the extent to which the enquiry is your own work
- the amount of direct help you have received beyond your normal entitlement

- the worth of the topic you have chosen to investigate and its sharpness of focus
- your awareness and understanding of the geography that is an integral part of the topic
- your appreciation of the context of, or background to, your topic
- the demonstration of your geographical skills, particularly your use of appropriate techniques for:
  - gathering information and data
  - analysing that data
  - interpreting the results
  - visually representing data, analyses and results
- your attitudes and values
- your ability to weigh up evidence, detect bias and reach conclusions based on analysis of the information and data you have collected
- your willingness to compile a report that does not exceed the word limit. Go over that limit and you do so at your peril!

From this list of possible assessment criteria you will appreciate that the personal enquiry has three particular emphases:

- on independent work
- on the use of skills
- on a focused pursuit of the chosen topic, be it a question, hypothesis, issue or problem.

SECTION C

Choosing your topic

As it is largely your choice, it is important that you select a topic that will stimulate and retain your interest. A good topic is one that is:

- **focused** – it zooms in on a particular question, issue, problem or hypothesis
- **valid** – it is geographical (it is concerned with spatial relationships) and relates to one or more of your A-level modules
- **manageable** – it can be properly investigated in the time available and reported upon within the prescribed word limit
- **viable** – it is possible to collect sufficient relevant data and information in the local area
- **exciting** – it raises your enthusiasm and doing it is not going to become a chore.

Although the amount of help you have received from your teachers is one of the criteria by which your enquiry might be assessed, you are entitled to consult with them over the selection of a topic. Indeed, they will expect to be consulted by you. Go along to them with some ideas and preferably more than one possible topic. You will only be penalised if they find it necessary to tell you what to do. In other words, their role is to support your work (particularly the choice of topic) by being reactive rather than proactive. They should not have to chase you to hand in your proposal form!

Do some background reading both before and after your early consultations with teachers. Be clear as to the geographical context of what you might like to investigate. You might also discuss your ideas with others in your group. Gradually, you need to arrive at a topic that satisfies the five criteria identified above. In order to give the whole thing a clear sense of purpose, you might express the title of your proposed topic in the form of a question.

Your exam board may require your choice of topic (and proposed methodology) to be approved by an external moderator. Take careful note of their remarks and comments. Moderators have a great deal of experience and are really trying to help you. Be prepared to redraft and resubmit your proposal if necessary.

SECTION D

Planning the investigation

Once you have been given the go-ahead on a topic, you need to plan carefully how you are going to undertake the enquiry. Most likely this will be a matter of fleshing out and refining ideas that you had when you discussed the topic with your teachers and when you submitted it for approval.

The key matters to be sorted out now are:

- What data do you need to collect?
- Where are you going to collect it?
- How are you going to collect it?

Dealing with these three issues will inevitably raise a whole of range of supplementary questions:

- Is any special equipment needed?
- Is such equipment available and if so where?
- Is the data needed for the investigation measurable and how?
- How much data needs to be collected, and in what way, to ensure that it represents a reliable sample?
- What steps need to be taken to rule out 'bias' in the investigation?
- Should any field tests or pilot studies be undertaken before beginning the actual enquiry?

Answering questions such as these should then allow you to draw up a work programme or timetable. This will set out the order in which you undertake particular parts of the investigation. Ideally, you should also set a deadline for the completion of each step. That programme and schedule should also be extended to take account of the next two stages in the enquiry, namely the analysis of your data and the presentation of your results.

SECTION E

Collecting the data

All personal enquiries require the collection of primary data, usually in the field through measurement, mapping, questionnaires, etc. and using random sampling techniques where appropriate. Observe critically and record your results carefully. Other evidence such as photographs and field sketches as well as the secondary information you need should also be gathered – population data from the Census or information about shops from trade directories, for example. Make sure the data collected is strictly relevant (not marginal) to your topic. Ensure that what you are collecting will enable you to answer your original question.

If you choose to investigate a topic in a location away from your home area, it is crucial that you prepare yourself properly. Be sure you know exactly what needs to be collected by way of data and that what you collect is accurate. You do not want to run the risk of having to make a lengthy return journey to check your facts or collect missing data.

Always keep your personal safety in mind. This is especially important if attempting a river or coastal study, or if working in upland areas, but some urban areas can be hazardous too. You may need someone to accompany you or to assist – if only to hold the other end of the tape measure! It is quite permissible for students to collect data jointly, provided that the theme of your study and the analysis and interpretation of the evidence is all your own.

SECTION F

Analysis and coming up with results

It is in the analysis of data that you have an opportunity to demonstrate your understanding of statistical techniques, but don't just use them to show off! You must keep your original aim clearly in mind. The techniques used should be chosen because they are relevant and show how the data and evidence answer your original question. You may wish to demonstrate certain characteristics of your data – its range by means of medians, quartiles and standard deviations, its clustering by nearest-neighbour analysis and location quotients, or its correlations by Spearman's rank coefficient and Chi-squared. You might also wish to check the significance of the data.

Remember that the techniques of analysis are not only statistical. Others available include graphs, diagrams, maps and photographs. There is a tension here that you need to resolve. On the one hand you want to demonstrate your awareness of, and competence with a range of techniques. On the other hand, you should use only those that are appropriate and central to your particular enquiry.

Having completed your analyses, the next step is to pull together all the results and interpret them. What conclusions do you draw and what bearing do these have on the question that you posed at the beginning of the enquiry?

SECTION G

Writing your report

The challenge now is to produce a report of your enquiry that is well structured and logically organised, clearly and concisely written. Perhaps the following outline might serve as model; at least it identifies some of the key points to be covered.

Introduction
- define and explain the topic
- justify its choice
- put it in a broader context

Data collection and analysis
- what data was collected and how
- reliability of data
- how data was analysed
- any problems at this stage

Results
- conclusions drawn
- how these relate to the original question
- acknowledge the limitations of the enquiry
- suggest how further enquiry might build on your findings

Be selective in what you report. It is very tempting to include everything that you have found out during the course of your enquiry, but resist this. Only include it if it is strictly relevant – it is quality, not quantity, that is required. Remember, there is a word limit.

SECTION H

Illustration

An important aspect of the report preparation and presentation is illustration. A sensible use of visual aids will greatly enhance the impact of your report. Basically that visual material is intended to do a number of things:

- convey impressions of the area studied and the data collected
- show the actual analyses that were central to the enquiry
- represent the more important findings or results.

Since geography is particularly concerned with spatial relationships and the differences between places, much of the data or information collected lends itself to mapping. Avoid simply redrawing or photocopying existing maps. They should always be adapted in some way to the requirements of your study. Remember, every map needs a key, scale and north point.

Your findings might also be presented on annotated cross-sections or transect diagrams. What about transparent or traced map overlays for demonstrating growth stages of a settlement or distribution of vegetation, land use and geology? Data can also be shown as proportional symbols or histograms located appropriately on maps. You may also wish to consider using scatter graphs, frequency diagrams, best-fit lines, rose diagrams, as well as pie, line, circular and triangular graphs. But make sure that the techniques you use are suited to the type of data and that they convey the messages that you want them to.

As with analytical techniques, you have to steer a careful course between showing that you are familiar with a whole range of different illustrative techniques and choosing only those that are best suited to the purposes of your report. There is a real danger of overkill here – be warned! As a general rule, every illustration you use should be made to earn its place in the report. If in doubt, chuck it out!

A final tip about your illustrations. Give each one a caption and a figure number. They should be presented and numbered according to the order in which they are referred to in the text. Do be sure to integrate the illustrations with the text. If you need any guidance as to how this is done, simply look at the way the two have been linked together in this book. Remember, if you do not make reference to an illustration in your text, the examiner will not bother to look at it. What a waste of your time and effort!

SECTION I

The finishing touches

Most examination boards require that the report of your enquiry is presented on A4 paper and secured within a pocket folder or file. You are also encouraged to use a word processor, but this is not mandatory.

When you have completed your report, set it aside for a few days. Then re-read it. Put yourself in the position of the examiner. Coming to it cold, does it make sense, is it always clear and easy to follow? Do a quick word-count – are you inside the word limit? If not, then look to do some pruning. Amend the draft as necessary and then proof-read it. That means check your spelling, punctuation and grammar, as well as the accuracy of your calculations and illustrations. Are those illustrations properly integrated with the text? Make any necessary corrections as neatly as possible. This is easily done if you have used a word processor for the text.

It is a fact of life that most people (and that includes examiners) are influenced by appearances. A neatly presented, well-bound, typed report with a title page, list of contents and carefully produced illustrations is going to create a very favourable impression with the person marking it. It will speak volumes about the qualities of the student. The simple message is this: do allow yourself sufficient time to add these finishing touches and to give your work a final polish.

Now you are probably ready to hand in your report – hopefully well before the final deadline!

SECTION J

Summing up

Planning is the key to a successful personal enquiry. Much of that planning is to do with time management. Once you have submitted your topic and had it approved – ideally well ahead of the deadline set by your teacher or the exam board – get on with it. You know what you have got to do. So ensure you have the time to do it. If you want to collect your data early on and spend a lot of time thinking about it before writing it up, then do so. But never spend a lot of time thinking about collecting data! That is a sure way of getting behind schedule. Let things slip and you will soon find yourself in the worst possible scenario. Having to cram everything into the last few weeks – data collection, analysis and writing up – is one of the easiest ways of throwing away marks. Be sure not to fritter away this golden opportunity to demonstrate your worth in circumstances that should lack the stress and tension of the examination room.

More advice on the personal enquiry can be found in a companion volume in the EPICS series, entitled *Skills and Techniques for Geography A-Level.*

CHAPTER

10 Making the grade

This is a summary of advice to be read just before your examinations. It is largely to do with exam technique. We hope that it will help to calm your nerves and put you in the positive state of mind that is required for performing well under examination conditions.

SECTION A

An acronym for the exam room

First, you need some sort of slogan or banner to carry with you into the examination room. Something to remind you what the examination is seeking to assess. The acronym **GRADE** may be useful.

G is for your **grasp** of **Geography** – your knowledge and understanding of its concepts, principles and theories.

R is for your ability to **read** (interpret) and **represent** geographical data in a variety of different forms – maps, diagrams, tables and photographs.

A is for your **ability** to **answer** questions directly and explicitly, and to **appreciate** their full implications, **acknowledging** the key commands of a question (more about that shortly).

D is for the **desirability** of **demonstrating** your powers of **deduction** – your ability to reason, argue a case, put together a coherent **discussion**.

E is for the **essential** nature of **examples** (including case studies) – to use them to support and **embellish** your answers.

Here in the five letters of GRADE we have identified some seven key skills. Perform satisfactorily in these skill areas and you will certainly make the grade you deserve.

SECTION B

The critical first 10 minutes

The first 10 minutes of an examination are absolutely critical. What you do then – the choices you make – can have a profound impact on the outcome of the whole exam.

There are many types of assessment used at A-level (**10.1**). It is vital that you know how each of your modules is assessed. In the case of unseen examination papers, it is equally important to know what type or types of question will appear in each paper. The last thing you want are any nasty surprises when you turn over the examination paper!

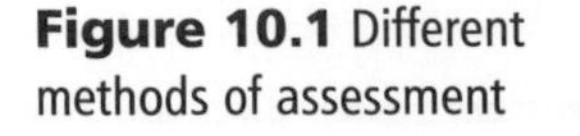

Figure 10.1 Different methods of assessment

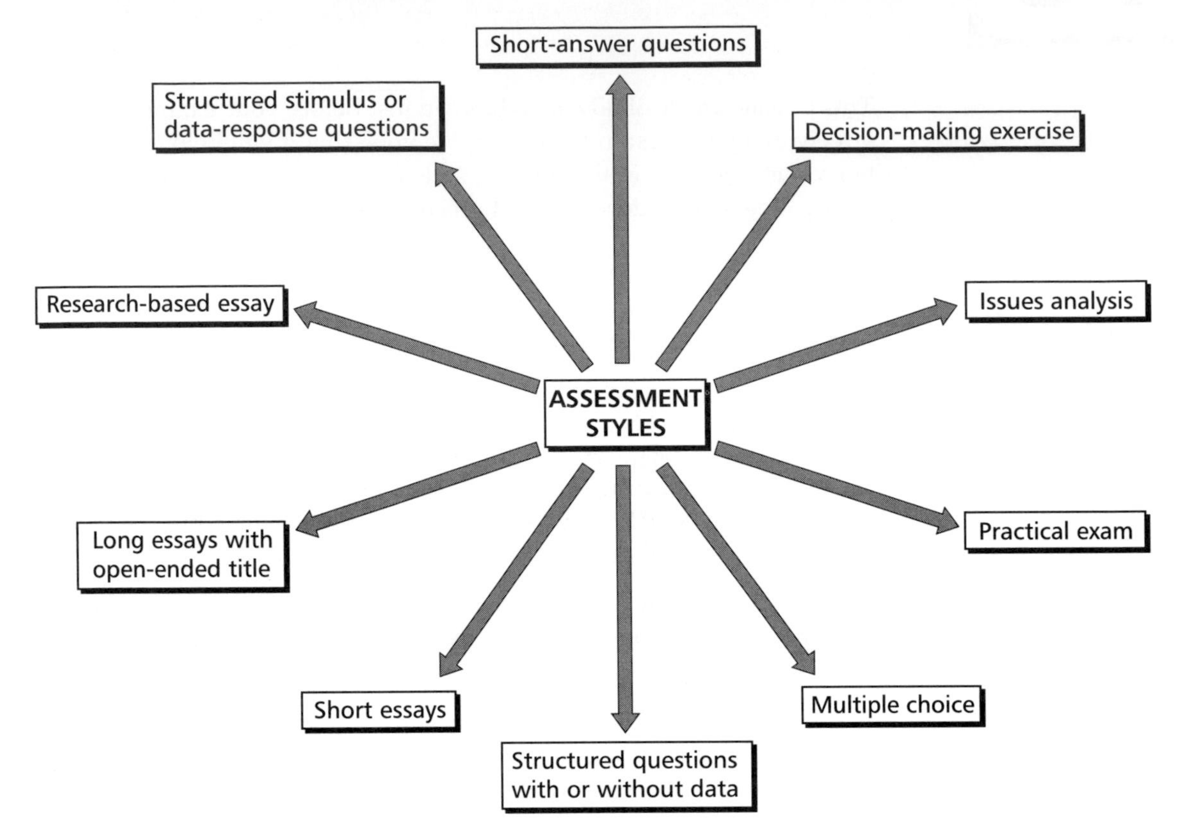

Rubric

First read the rubric – that is, the set of instructions at the head of the questions paper. Some papers have a complex rubric and it is a very good idea to have a look at the most recent so that you know exactly what the format is. Double-check:

- the number of questions that have to be attempted
- how the required number of questions have to be selected from the various sections that make up the paper
- whether all the questions carry equal marks
- the amount of time you have.

Time

On this last point, a tip. Well before the start of the examination period, work out a timetable for each paper. First subtract at least 10 minutes from the total time. You need this time to read the paper, select the questions you are going to tackle, and read through all your answers at the end of the exam. Then divide the remainder by the number of questions. It is vital that you give each question roughly the amount of time and attention that is proportional to the marks on offer. In most papers, all questions carry equal marks, but you will need to check this. Having found out how much time you have for each question, work out the exact times when you should be finishing one question and starting the next (these are your **move-on** or **get-a-move-on times**). Memorise them just before you go into the exam room. Take a watch or small travelling clock in with you.

Question selection

Now read through the whole of the exam paper calmly and carefully and start to make your question selection. As you do so, check that are satisfying the rubric requirements. It is tempting to have your choice of question triggered by the occurrence of familiar terms – 'plate tectonics', 'global warming', 'location quotient', 'urban models' and so on. It is very natural to make a grab for such questions, but double-check that you are absolutely sure exactly what the question is asking. Can you really cope? Can you come up with the goods? Do you have relevant examples and case-study material at your disposal? Re-read the paper and make sure that you did not overlook a more 'friendly' question that better suits the knowledge, understanding and supportive materials that you have.

In the case of data-response questions, don't be put off by the stimulus material. Cartoons or sketches can look far more user-friendly than complex graphs and maps, but you need to look at the difficulty-level of the whole question.

Always choose questions from the sections of the syllabus that your centre has studied (most syllabuses have options). You are unlikely to do so well recalling your GCSE knowledge or your General Studies project, for example.

This double-checking of question choice – of being sure that you have chosen the questions that best suit you – is a vital aspect of successful examination technique.

Answer planning

Having made an initial selection of questions, do some outline planning. Brainstorm the questions (see **Chapter 3, Section A**) and for each come up with a simple structure to order your points, checking as you do so that you have appropriate case-study material. Are you still happy with your question choice? Are you clear about the command words of the question?

SECTION C

Command words

Always check what you are being asked to do before launching into writing your answer. Underline the key words, in particular focusing on those common command words that usually start a question. Make sure you do as you are asked.

- **Account for** = explain the cause of
- **Analyse** = take apart and show how the component parts interrelate
- **Annotate** = put notes on (usually a diagram) to pinpoint key features
- **Assess** = weigh up, look at the pluses and minuses
- **Comment** = write explanatory notes
- **Compare** = point out similarities and differences
- **Contrast** = differences only, but in both cases (compare and contrast) you must write an integrated account, i.e. 'in x… whereas in y…'
- **Discuss** = present the arguments for and against an issue – you can give your own opinion at the end or, even better, a summarised overview
- **Evaluate** = estimate the value of, but weigh up the importance of; or look at pros and cons
- **Explain** = give reasons for
- **Illustrate** = give an example, a case study, a map or diagram
- **Justify** = present a valid argument or support a decision saying why, but also why not
- **Outline** = give the main details or general principles
- **Review** = make a survey of and look at the points critically
- **State** = make a number of brief points
- **Suggest** = give a range of responses; it may be that there is no one definite answer
- **Summarise** = state the main features of an argument
- **To what extent?** = you have to review the value of an argument, perhaps avoiding the complete acceptance of it

SECTION D

Timing

You have already worked out how much time you have for each question.

Make sure you do the full number of questions and complete them. This is vitally important in short modular exams where you are required to answer two questions in $1\frac{1}{2}$ hours. If you only complete questions, you can lose 25 per cent of the marks, as you do not get marks for what you have not attempted. It is always worth trying to finish in coherent note form if you don't have time to write the answer out properly. If you have done a plan for an answer, do not cross it out until you have finished. If you run out of time, the examiner might be able to find a small amount of credit for your ideas written in the plan.

Pace yourself by looking at the marks down the side of the question paper. These are known as weightings. For example, in a 25 mark question which should take you 45 minutes in all, if part (a) is worth 9 marks and part (b) is worth 16 marks, you clearly need only spend around 15 minutes on part (a).

Match the length of your answers to the weightings. As a rough rule, multiply the weightings by 3, i.e. for 9 marks, write a minimum of 27 lines (average-sized writing).

Plan your answers, but only draw up a brief plan. Unless you are doing a formal lengthy essay or a decision-making exercise, never spend more than 5 to 10 per cent of the time on planning.

Master an effective style of presentation, with careful handwriting and diagrams. Remember that when you write against time, your presentation will be under pressure. It will hold up if you have practised enough.

Learn not to waste words. You need to practise writing exam answers where every word counts and the prose is packed with geographical facts.

Use diagrams and maps effectively. They take time to produce, but with useful annotations they can actually save time in the end.

Allow 5 minutes at the end of the examination for a quick read-through and review of your work.

SECTION E

Support from the real world

On the front of most A-level papers is a note to the effect that credit will be given for the appropriate use of examples. Do you remember how an example is different from a case study? What does 'appropriate' mean? There is no doubt that inappropriate case studies can lead to disaster.

An **example** means that you should write two or three sentences to illustrate a point. When writing about the distribution of corries (cirques), you might state that:

> *A study of the Lake District shows that 60 per cent of corries are found facing north-east (for example Red Tarn near Helvellyn) and that these corries tend to be much larger. South-facing corries are very rare and tend only to occur at very high altitudes (for example Stickle Tarn).*

Case studies usually allow you to carry out an in-depth description to illustrate a whole range of points (see **Chapter 5**). You can prepare a whole set of case studies with the help of your teacher, the syllabus and an analysis of past papers, but you have to be prepared to tailor them to fit the demands of the question set.

Don't forget:

- Get the right length – look at the marks.
- Get the balance between breadth and depth – check whether you are asked for **one** or a **range of** case studies
- Get the scale correct – the local stream is **not** 'a large drainage basin', nor is the Amazon rainforest 'a small ecosystem'.
- Get the specification correct – often you need to select a city in an ELDC and Liverpool will not do! Coalmining is not a manufacturing industry.

- Fill your case study with facts, statistics and precise locations. A sketch map or diagram can save many words, provided it is really linked to the question.
- Always look for original case studies based on your own fieldwork and practical studies, but write them up just like any other and not as a personal diary.

Finally, always remember to put some real world into your answers. There is nothing so sterile as a wholly abstract answer. You will certainly miss out on credit if you fail to come up with supporting examples and case studies.

SECTION F

Skills – a checklist

During an A-level Geography course, especially one of the newer modular courses, you will have to develop a significant range of skills, some general and some geographical. Make a checklist as you go through the course and use this as a revision guide to ensure that you have looked over all the skills you may be asked to use in the examination. These include the following.

- Analysing OS and other maps. If you follow some syllabuses, you are allowed to use a special examination atlas, and you need to spend some time before the exam familiarising yourself with it to see how you could use it to enhance your answers.
- Analysing satellite images, photographs and sketches.
- Evaluating cartoons and articles.
- Summarising and analysing information in a table.
- Annotating maps and diagrams.
- Drawing effective sketch maps and diagrams of your own.
- Interpreting graphs and statistical data.
- Assessing opinions and values.

SECTION G

Some final *dos* and *don'ts*

Finally, it might be helpful if we could assemble much of the advice given in this and earlier chapters into yet another simple acronym, something to take with you into the examination room. Bearing in mind the need for a positive state of mind, the word **SCORE** seems a good one to use as a reminder of the things we should do.

S Do **study** the question paper **slowly** and carefully.
Do **select** your questions carefully.
Do **see** all **sides** of the question.

C Do **confine** your answers to the spaces provided in any answer book.
Do **check** that you have answered all parts of the question and the required number of questions.
Do **construct** a **coherent**, **concise** and **convincing** response.
Do **capitalise** on appropriate case studies.

O Do **observe** the command words in questions.
Do **organise** your thoughts and arguments before starting an answer.

R Do **read** the **rubric** and follow its instructions.
Do **remain relevant** to the question.

E Do **ensure** an **equal** or appropriate allocation of time and **effort** to all questions.
Do **exemplify** and illustrate.
Do **exploit** supporting case studies.

There are also some *don'ts* – things to avoid if you wish to pass the examinations with flying colours. Again we might put this 'negative' advice in the form of another acronym. The word **WASTE** serves the purpose well.

W Don't **waffle**.
Don't **write illegibly**.

A Don't **answer by allusion** – that is, leave the examiner to draw their own conclusions from a mass of ill-targeted and badly organised material.

S Don't **set your own question**.
Don't **spray the grapeshot** in the hope that something you write might be relevant.

T Don't **trot out rehearsed answers** that may or may not have anything to do with this year's questions.
Don't **try the examiner's patience**.

E Don't **end your answers** with 'Thus it can be seen ...' – because most times it cannot!
Don't **expect the examiner to exude** goodwill if you fail to observe all these don'ts!

So now you are on your own. Good luck! You won't need it, if by the time you come to the examination you have followed the advice in this book, and during the examinations you heed the guidance given in this last chapter. By these means you will make the grade that you really deserve.

Acknowledgements

With thanks to the following for permission to reproduce photographs and other copyright material in this book:

Edexcel Foundation, pages 43–44, Figs 7.13, 8.2, 8.3, 8.4;
Hodder & Stoughton, Fig. 8.1.

Frank Lane Picture Agency, Fig. 7.9.

Every effort has been made to contact copyright holders. The publishers apologise to anyone whose rights have been inadvertently overlooked, and will be happy to rectify any errors or omissions.